MARKETING ONLINE, CLEAR AND SIMPLE

HOW TO CREATE INCOME USING THE INTERNET

IN COMMERCE TODAY, YOU OPERATE IN TWO UNIVERSES;
DISCOVER HERE HOW TO OPERATE IN THE ONLINE UNIVERSE.

BY *ARTHUR CRONOS, BA*

WWW.COPYDRAGON.COM

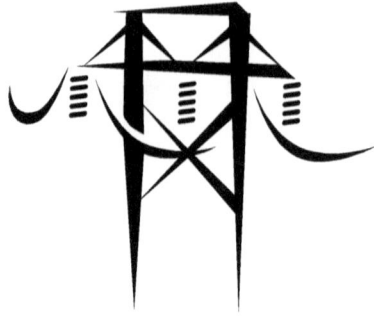

Powerline Press
1445 Ieka Street
Weed, CA 96094 USA
(530) 938-1100

www.CopyDragon.com

PUBLISHER'S NOTE:

This book is sold subject to the condition that it shall not, by way of trade or otherwise, be lent, re-sold, hired out, or otherwise circulated without the publisher's prior consent in any form of binding or cover other than that in which it is published and without a similar condition including this condition being imposed on the subsequent purchaser.

"Things should be as simple as possible, but no simpler." — *Albert Einstein*

DISCLAIMER:

Every effort has been made to make this guide as complete and accurate as possible. Although the author and publisher have made every effort to ensure accuracy, there may be mistakes in typography or content. The author and the publisher do not warrant that the information contained in this report is fully complete and shall not be responsible for any errors or omissions. The author and publisher shall have neither liability nor responsibility to any person or entity with respect to any loss or damage caused or alleged to be caused directly or indirectly by this report.

The purpose of this report is educational, with the intent to provide information to help you apply business principles and methods as described. Because this report contains information on marketing and technology only up to the publishing date, this information should be used as a guide – not as the ultimate source of Internet marketing information. Before you begin, check with the appropriate authorities to insure compliance with applicable laws and regulations.

Arthur Cronos
CopyDragon webwriters – commercial writing/marketing agency
1445 Ieka Street
Weed, CA 96094
(530) 938-1100
arthur@copydragon.com

PREFACE

"If there's no time for the things you love, then do the things you love exist anywhere in time? If they don't exist anywhere in time, then are you having anything you love in your life? If not, why not change time? — Richard French

---

All my life I have been fascinated by the mind, its unconscious activities, the creative drive, and how to apply creative efforts to one's life ... to have a productive and happy life.

I learned how to hypnotize my young friends when I was thirteen, and never stopped studying the mind and its mysteries. After college days I travelled and had adventures, and eventually settled in San Francisco and became interested in business. That is, I became fascinated by sales and marketing and how these activities involve both the conscious and the so-called unconscious mind.

In college days, I'd yearned to be a writer, and in sales and marketing (and advertising) I began to discover how good writing makes a huge difference in business. Because nothing much happens in a business until you learn to get some sales. And selling is mostly done through words.

Over the next 40 years, the way you use words didn't change a lot. But *where* you use the words changed tremendously.

When I began running my own businesses – a bookkeeping service, an advertising service, an answering service, a detective agency, a voicemail company – the most common forms of advertising for a small local business included printed brochures, newspaper and yellow-pages advertisements, and sometimes things like posters, and radio, and lots of networking face to face. Presentations were mostly face-to-face, or on the telephone.

But over these 40 years, new forms of communication appeared, and *where* you used those words moved into these new communication spaces: into email, into downloadable documents and videos and audio files, into web pages, into cell-phone conversations and instant messaging and webinars.

The face of business changed. The words were still needed. But they underwent change along with the communication space. For example, on a webpage your visitors won't wait long, and so your words must get to the point faster.

The same principles apply, but *how* you apply them, and *where*, changed.

As it happened, in my businesses I worked with the telephone system. For example, I had designed equipment for our answering service which interacted with the telephone company switching system. And as it happened, the Internet is a development that grew out of the telephone network, so the early Internet made sense to me.

And as it happened, again simply by chance, I was an early adopter of the first "micro-computers." My first computer was a solder-it-yourself computer with a whopping 64K of memory, and there were almost no commercial programs, so I learned to write (code) our own programs for managing a mailing list, for bookkeeping, and for controlling machinery.

I remember a trip on my motorcycle one evening, down the peninsula to attend the regular monthly meeting of the "Homebrew Computer Club," where I saw two scruffy guys named Steve demonstrating a color-board for their new "Apple" computer. They looked like me in my hippy days, and I figured they'd never make it in this new computer world. Ha!

The point is: when these computers began developing rapidly, I was fascinated, and when developments in transistors, small computers, and the telephone network that became known as the Internet started to become generally known – and adopted by business – I was fascinated to try "selling in the Cyber Universe."

Now, 40 years later, business in general has adopted this new Universe. And because I've been doing commercial writing and marketing all this time, for my own businesses and for the many other companies who hired me, it's time to share what I've discovered.

Because it's a wilderness out there, a stupefying avalanche of information – some true, and some completely bogus – and although any local business person suspects that they should be doing *something* on the Internet, the question is ... What? How?

I didn't intend to acquire this information, but simply due to circumstance, I've had the good fortune to see how selling and writing is adapted to the Cyber-Universe. And through working with my clients and their businesses, I've discovered how to separate what works from the tidal wave of opinions and methods that normally bury the inquiring business person.

So it's time to share what I've discovered.

May it simplify your life, and help you to live the life you always wanted.

— *Arthur Cronos*

September 6, 2011
Weed, California USA

Bonus: Free How-to Videos for Amazon, Nook, and iBook Buyers

"The limiting factor of what you can accomplish is the mind. If you can see it in your mind, you can do it." -- Arnold Schwartzenegger

---

How to get the Free How-to Videos that Illustrate this Book

In this book, I'll describe how a local business can use the power of the Internet to find new customers, and to increase sales from existing customers.

I'll describe in full the "Three-Step Marketing" approach developed by CopyDragon webwriters, a professional business writing and marketing design firm. This approach is easy to understand, makes clear what needs to be done and in what order, and applies equally to marketing in the physical universe and the cyber universe.

Finally, we'll present an actual "nuts and bolts" explanation, step-by-step details of how to create an online website which will powerfully attract customers, how to engage those visitors into an ongoing conversation, and how to increase the traffic to your website.

Seeing is Believing

For most of us, seeing a real example makes learning easier, so we have created a companion video series. And to assist your learning, we provide these videos at no cost to purchasers of this book, in an exclusive "Members Area" on our book website.

Please go to http://MarketingOnlineClearAndSimple.com, where it will offer to sell you the videos, along with a pdf download of this book, readable on any computer.

But since you have already purchased this book on Amazon or elsewhere, you can register for FREE access to the videos in the Members Area, and you'll get a free copy of the pdf book as well.

Please see the "Resource section" of this book for the "coupon code" that will make your access to the videos free.

TABLE OF CONTENTS

INTRODUCTION

"Buddha Is as Buddha Does." — *Richard French.*

THE PREACHER'S METHOD

As the story goes, there was a preacher in the south who gave great sermons, and everybody got real excited, and what's more, after the service many of them could actually recall parts of what had been said.

Remarking on this unusual situation, one of the preacher's good friends asked him his secret that enabled his parishioners to actually recall things that he said. According to the preacher's reply, he had a three-part formula, which was —

1. **First I tells 'em what I'm goinna tell 'em**

2. **Then I tells 'em**

3. **Then I tells 'em what I done told 'em**

So in this spirit, here is what you are going to learn in this book:

THE OUTLINE OF THIS BOOK

A) I'll give an overview of the easy-to-understand "Three-Step Marketing" formula we developed at CopyDragon webwriters; and then

B) I'll give detailed how-to instructions on how to apply the formula step-by-step to create new income for your local business by using the power of the Internet.

THE "DESTINATION" APPROACH

Now, let's say you have a plan. You have a destination and you want to get to the other side of a forest. Well, before worrying about how to cross this creek and how to get around this big tree, it's a pretty good idea to know in which direction the destination lies, and to have a general plan for getting across the forest.

The way this particular book is structured is like this. First I'll overview the two universes – the physical universe and the cyber universe – and the Three-Step Marketing formula, so you will have a clear idea how this simple three-step process can be used for marketing either in the real world or in the cyber universe.

In this way, your existing knowledge of the real world will help you understand this process when applied to the cyber universe.

And then, for the cyber universe, we'll break each of these three steps down into a step-by-step formula for how to go about setting up (a) your location online, (b) your conversation system(s) which will engage your visitor, and finally (c) how to create traffic, meaning to cause visitors to come to your website.

WHAT YOU'LL TAKE AWAY

- First is that there are two universes in which you **_must_** operate these days.

- Second is that 20 percent of all the information you *could* learn is going to give you 80 percent of the results, and so we'll simply focus on a tested 20% that will give you a big advantage over your competition.

- Third is that there really is a way of looking at marketing that involves only three steps, and it's the same three steps in the same order whether it's the real universe or the cyber universe.

The focus here is that you will have a clear vision of how to move forward step-by-step using the Three-Step Marketing formula to generate income from the cyber universe.

Marketing Online for a Local Business

"A little unlearning goes a long way." — *Richard Kehl*

Why Local Businesses Struggle to Get Online

Local business owners generally suspect they could get more business if they could somehow tap into the power of the Internet. After all, many companies make millions on the Internet, so why not Joe's Hardware in Des Moines, Iowa?

The Ugly Facts

Fact: Almost no local business owner ever figures out how to make it work.

Why not? What gets in the way?

First, the entire marketing focus, and the entire product delivery of a local business is to customers in the local area. The product or the service is delivered right there, not out in cyberspace. It's all very well for Dell Computer to accept an order on the Internet, and ship out that computer, but how can Joe at Joe's hardware do that? It's very, very complicated, and what's worse, it's endlessly changing.

There is no way that Joe will undertake this project, and if he did – unless he's very gifted – the solution is probably beyond his available time. Especially since he's generally very busy, juggling tasks, helping people, dealing with the government, paperwork, advertising, ordering, stocking, hiring/firing/training, upgrading his existing cash-register/inventory system, analyzing to stay on top of what's most profitable, and plugging leaks and fixing problems, all done in a limited amount of time, day after day.

His business isn't Internet marketing. It's running a hardware store on main street. It's just not feasible to learn another, completely different business ...

... unless ...

... somebody comes along, where marketing online *is* their business – but they've been running local businesses for years – and this person extracts the principles that have been tested and known to work, and then boils it down to a simple set of steps, that a normal human could actually follow.

And that's exactly what I've done here, in this book.

Oh, we're not going to build a system like Dell Computer for Joe's Hardware. Because for Joe's business, that's not where the money is. For Joe's business, the successful action is to establish a foothold in this new universe (cyberspace) where a lot of people spend a lot of time.

And if Joe does the right steps in the cyber universe, he can find new customers, have an automatic system to engage them in a conversation (that will lead to sales), and there are things he can do that cause more and more people to visit his online presence, get into the conversation, and decide to buy from Joe.

Now realize that the way most of us begin our thinking about Internet marketing ... is just plain wrong. What we generally do is this: We see that some business has a website, and we think, "I gotta get a website."

Oops. Because you can "get a website," and most of the businesses that do ... don't make a dime.

Because, as you will discover in the pages of this book, having a website is only the first of three necessary steps, *and* that website needs to be built the right way in the first place if it's to do you any good. Further, it's the other two steps that turn a website into a money-generating machine.

Any business owner running a local business can if he/she wishes, apply the "Three-Step Marketing" formula described in this book, step by step. If you *only* get the first step done – creating a website in the correct manner – you will have made a major step forward.

And when you complete the second two steps, you'll discover new customers, new income flowing through your doors, and a delightfully automatic new way to boost your income.

WHAT THIS BOOK CAN DO FOR YOU

"Outside of a dog, a book is man's best friend. Inside of a dog, it's too dark to read." — Groucho Marx

---

It will help you if you understand how we came to have two universes in which we must operate, in commerce today. You'll better understand how to operate in the physical universe, and you'll understand how to use the Internet to increase your income, even if you are a local business, serving local customers.

So let's look at how this two-universe situation evolved …

THE EVOLUTION OF TWO UNIVERSES FOR COMMERCE

A couple of hundred years ago in the USA, there were trails and there were trappers and hunters moving along these trails and into the wilderness and plains, searching for animals like beaver and muskrat and buffalo for hides and such.

Along those trails, merchants would set up trading posts, and those that were well-situated would see the emergence of villages, towns and cities, and more merchants would come there to do business.

The way you did business was you went and talked to somebody. Go over their house. Go over their place of business. Talk to them face to face. If you owed them a piece of information, you might have Johnny take them a note or letter.

Benjamin Franklin had a bright idea. He thought it was a good idea to have post offices so someone else would carry your letter.

A fellow named Sears came across a real good deal on watches in Chicago, and bought hundreds of them. How is he going to sell them? He decided to sell them by mail. Later on, he got a partner named Roebuck. They did real well.

Catalog selling flourished. It was a new way of communicating. The customer didn't have to go to the store anymore. It's as if the seller's words and sometimes pictures came to the customer.

ELECTRICITY

Now, in 1940, we had the Rural Farm Electrification Act and farms across America got light bulbs, radios and telephones. The telephone had already been invented. It was big in cities but after the Rural Farm Electrification Act it was pretty much universal.

Traveling salesmen began to dwindle because it was easier to call. You couldn't call long distance at first, but most business was still done in town.

When I was a child, I saw the old-fashioned phone which hung on the wall change to the candle-stick phone, and then to the tabletop phone. There was no touch tone pad. There was no rotary dial. You talked to Mabel and Mabel would connect you to Sally Smith's house. As the phones expanded rapidly, the phone company invented switching machines for phone company central offices, those windowless offices you can see in every town.

The first switching machines had bars and levers and that was called crossbar ... but in Bell Labs, they had invented a thing called a transistor, better than a vacuum tube, smaller, less power, more reliable, lasted longer and more sturdy.

These things [transistors] first went into audio applications, radio, later television, and switching equipment. The switching equipment for the phone company was then called "ESS" for electronic switching system and later on "Digital" when it was controlled by a computer.

Finally, calculators. I remember the first affordable calculator. It was about the size of a paperback book. It was from a company named Litronix. It cost less than $100. How can they do that?

I bought one, and started a bookkeeping business.

Someone in New Mexico was also looking at these developing calculator chips and realized a certain chip had all the parts that a computer needs. It was a chip called the 8008. The Altair, a kind of a homebrew computer, appeared.

THE INTERNET

Now we've got computers and we've got a phone system and luckily at that point, the Department of Defense in the 60's became convinced that we were all going to be bombed by nuclear missiles out of Russia. And that might knock out the phone system.

The phone system already works in a flexible way. You call your aunt. If they can't send the call through Los Angeles, they will send it through Denver.

But the military is way more concerned about reliable communications, no matter what bothersome bombs may fall. The military guys said, "Well, yes, the phone company routing is flexible. But then after you're talking to someone far away, if that line gets bombed, then you would lose the connection. So let's chop it up into little bits and we'll send them all sorts of different ways and reassemble at the other end."

That Department of Defense project was called ARPANET. We know it these days as the Internet.

It was bankrolled by the government … and so the military was asked to share it with the universities. The university guys, they're passing papers back and forth. A guy in Switzerland says, "Gosh, these things are boring. Wouldn't it be great instead of a big page of text if you could have like a headline and maybe a subheading and maybe a picture? Oh, I know. I'll just put a little something in the text file to label things. So this is the headline. This is a subheading. This is a picture."

Can you say webpage?

Now in parallel, we have a phone system – the Internet is a spin-off of the phone system – we have transistors fueling computers, and then Steve Jobs and Steve Wozniak at Apple stole Alan Kay's Palo Alto Dynabook graphical interface so that Bill Gates at Microsoft could steal it from them.

PERSONAL COMPUTERS WITH GRAPHICAL DISPLAY

I saw these two guys named Steve, who would create Apple Computer, one evening in the lobby of the Stanford Linear Accelerator Center at the regular monthly meeting of the Homebrew Computer Club. They were showing a type of color board with flashing colors, and I said, "Those guys are never going to amount to anything." Oops. I was *so* wrong. Those two hippies changed our world!

The appearance and evolution of the world-wide web was in a way inevitable at this point. Because the graphical display ... plus the Internet system ... and folks owning computers made possible from the transistors that had been invented by the phone company ... these three things made surfing the web possible.

Businesses found it useful. Email was cheaper and quicker than a letter. We use email for the same reason today.

And very quickly, businesses figured, "Wait a minute. If I print my four-page colored brochure, it will cost me $4000 but I could put up 87 pages on the Internet and I never have to reprint them."

The first webpages were brochures.

THE WEB IS A UNIVERSE

A webpage and the web have, to our senses, all the appearance of the universe.

Here's a physical universe, all around us. It has got matter. There's energy. There's space and time.

When you're surfing the web, do you not have much the same experience? There are objects. Stuff is moving, that's energy. There seems to be space. You go from here to there … and there's a passage of time.

Now we can't touch it … yet.

And we don't see it in 3D … yet.

But our children or grandchildren probably will.

As an experience, it has all the elements of a universe.

Let's make an example. Let's take your father. Your father decided he was going to go into business and start the Rubber Chicken Store of Des Moines. He was going to specialize in rubber chickens, and maybe branch out into rubber hotdogs and rubber turkeys.

He's going to get a storefront. There are going to be customers. He's going to sell rubber chickens. End of story. He succeeds, or he fails.

But think: Today, if a person in Des Moines is going to look for rubber chickens, in which universe will they search?

The answer is: on the Internet.

It doesn't have more information, but it sure is quicker to get it.

I can think of exceptions. Maybe the drive-through espresso cart … maybe they don't need to be on the internet. But I think they might do better with a one-page website. Some people might want to look and see when they're open or where they are.

And I also have a friend who has a farm. He grows several fields full of hay every year. He places one small $25 classified in the local newspaper, and then immediately sells all the hay that he has. So clearly, he has no need of a website.

But are *you* in this situation? Are you already selling as much as possible with no website? (And if you are already that successful, then why are you reading this book?)

YOU MAY NOT HAVE AN OPTION: LOCATION

If you're selling products or services today, you probably do not have an option. You probably cannot fully succeed if you attempt to operate *only* in the physical universe.

Now let's look at it the other way around: You could have an *online-only* business – BlueNecktiesRUs.com – but you're still going to have to have an office in the physical universe where you can make or receive shipments of blue neckties.

Most likely, you don't really have an option. If you're not on the Internet, in some ways to the public, you just don't exist. You don't seem as legitimate. You're just not as solid.

Now, the reason I bring this up is because there really are Two Universes and the same three major actions or three steps will market in each one. It looks different, but they're the same three steps. I'll describe them shortly.

20% GETS 80% OF THE RESULTS

Who has ever seen this rule before?

"20% gets 80% of the Results"

Going back to this formula for three-step marketing, I can't claim too much credit because I stumbled into it. As it happens, every one of us has a certain path and you study this and this, but not that, and you meet this person, but not that one. You have this competency and that interest, but not these others.

In my case, I was interested in the unconscious mind. I learned how to hypnotize people at age thirteen. I've been studying the unconscious mind, therapy, and the way the mind works ever since.

When I got into business – after being a dope-smoking hippie for a while – I was fascinated with sales and marketing. Don't know why. I was a lousy businessman in some way. I didn't manage money very well but sales and marketing, I really liked that, and did well at it. In fact, on this subject I've been the featured speaker at trade conventions, and one of my early businesses is mentioned in the first two Guerilla Marketing books. I *really* enjoyed sales and marketing.

Something else: Another of my early businesses was answering service, later voicemail service. And in San Francisco, I was an early adaptor of computers, so I was very familiar both with the phone system and those early computers. I even built machine-control systems that worked with the phone company switching system.

Now because of these interests, over the last 40 years I've done commercial writing, and since the Internet appeared, I've used websites, building over 200 of them. I have dozens of clients that I work for as well. This experience has led me to select what I believe is the workable 20 percent of all the hoopla, bogus stuff and stuff that might or might not work.

In other words, these are the things that worked for me and my clients repeatedly. Now this approach isn't everything that might work. For example, I know a young lady who developed a great Facebook system, and that's a pathway I overlooked for a long time.

Because there can be variations, that's why this book is organized to give you an overall plan *first*, because the pieces can be different. What you'll find here is an outline of the pieces that are most often successfully used. But like a builder who can read an architect's drawings, when you understand the plan, you can better implement the system with understanding, to get the best results.

THE HAPPY-LIFE FORMULA

"Every day is a good day." — *Yun-Men*

WHAT TO DO *BEFORE* YOU START YOUR BUSINESS

When you're thinking about a business, you ***do not*** want to leap into action. First, you want to carefully think about, "What is the life I want to have?"

If you don't do this first, you may build a business that interferes with you getting the life you want to have. Don't laugh. It happens to thousands of people every day.

DESCRIBE THE LIFE YOU WANT

First, you start with, "What is the life I want to have?" and describe it in great detail. Think about what you want to spend your time doing, how much time, what you want for your family life, where you want to live, how much money you want to make and how much time you'll invest to make it.

If you don't plan your life, you'll get whatever life develops pretty much by accident. Odds are, that's not the life you'll best enjoy.

DESCRIBE THE BUSINESS THAT PROVIDES THAT LIFE

Once you have the life specification, you make a very detailed and accurate description of exactly the business that will give you that precise life.

Include: Single location or multiple locations? Employees? Contractors? Travel? How much gross income, estimated expenses, net profit? How much time must you spend to earn that net profit? What will you spend your time doing? What is the product you provide? What's your position in the market?

Now be careful. If you don't enjoy travelling in your perfect life, then for gosh sakes don't create a business that will require you to go travelling. Makes sense?

WHAT ARE THE STRATEGIC OBJECTIVES?

Once you have a detailed description of your business in the fullness of time to give you the life you want, then it's pretty easy.

"OK, I'm here," you say, "And over there is the business in the fullness of time." You can see this clearly.

So now you ask yourself: "What are the **strategic objectives** that I *must have accomplished* between here and there?"

WORK BACKWARDS

It's easy to work backwards. If your perfect business has three locations, Rubber Chickens in Des Moines, Dallas, and Denver, then obviously one of your strategic objectives has got to be that you establish a first location, then add a second and a third.

If you wanted to be a traveling hypnotherapist and you wanted to go to these seven cities, one of your first ones is, "Well, let's see if I can do that here, and then I'll go to one of those cities." You can start mapping it out. It becomes very clear and easy.

DESCRIBING YOUR TARGET CUSTOMER

Once you have your detailed business description, and those strategic objectives, you can specify your target customer.

- Is that customer male or female?

- How much money does he or she make?

- Are they married?

- Do they have children?

- What magazines does that person read?

- What television shows?

- What kind of car do they drive?

- Most important, what is the occupation?

The occupation gives you a direct view into the psychodrama that person is living out.

PSYCHODRAMA: MYTHS, FAIRY TALES, AND LEGENDS

I'll give you an example. Say we've got a banker. That's your target customer. Let's say you're selling cars. Start talking about respect, and if you want to draw a picture or tell a story, describe how it's kind of like the days back in the ancient mead hall when the patriarch would sit at the table and enjoy the admiration of all the young warriors around him.

Now the banker will actually respond to this because it's the life story he's living out, becoming the respected head of an organization, and he wants status, solid strength, and power.

Now let's consider a crop duster. You're going to sell him a motorcycle. You might start telling stories – You know, back in the Old West sometimes, a stranger would come into town. He did what he could to improve things and then he moved on, and you may find yourself feeling a little bit restless. When you do, you go outside and you just hop on this BMW XR-36 motorcycle, and you can roar up the road in a cloud of dust!

Tell that story to the banker. Where will you get? Nowhere.

Tell the mead hall story to the crop duster. Where will you get? Nowhere.

Occupation provides a real good window into the myths and legends that will appeal to your target customer. When you think about the myths and legends that they're already living out, then you know how to talk to that person. You also know what kind of colors they like. You can do it very intuitively and very simply.

There are also scientific studies, but a very simple and powerful method will be given in this book.

CHANGES OVER TIME? REVIEW!

Realize that if you had a vision five or eight years ago then quite possibly you have achieved it or you're on your way. But what if – today – you're actually wanting a little bit of a different life …

Then you have to change the plan.

You have to go back to the drawing board and say, "OK, now what do I want to do?"

TOP-DOWN PLANNING

As your life changes, now and then you will want to go back and then recreate top-down: life, business, objectives, customer.

You need to first define your desired life and then the business that matches carefully. For example if you happen to choose a life where you don't want to work seven days a week, and you're building yourself a business that regularly requires you to work seven days a week … then you're working against who?

You'd be working against *yourself*.

And who's the most powerful person that can get in your way?

It isn't them. It's you.

Even when it seems like it's them, it's only with your agreement. You are an infinite, spiritual being walking around temporarily in a meat body on this planet at this time. You are actually more powerful than you dream.

And everything that has ever happened to you, some of it just happened, and you either carry it around because you do; and it's you carrying it … or you have thrown it off, because you can.

THE THREE-STEP MARKETING FORMULA

"Thinking is more interesting than knowing, but less interesting than looking." — Goethe

---

THREE-STEP MARKETING: LOCATION, CONVERSATION, TRAFFIC

I sum up the Three-Step Marketing formula with these keywords:

1. First there's LOCATION. That's what you have to set up first.

2. And then there's CONVERSATION, meaning, "How do you engage someone who's just passing by or visiting briefly into an on-going conversation?"

3. Third is: "How do you get people to come? TRAFFIC."

Now, you might think, "Well, you got to have traffic coming in to your location first," but you can't do that until you have a location to send them to.

If you have your location, then you could generate traffic and then have a conversation … but if you generate the traffic without having a conversation system in place, they're going to come, and if they don't engage in conversation, they're going to leave, never to be seen again.

HOW MANY VISITS DOES IT TAKE TO BUY?

There's an organization in New York City. It's called the DMA, Direct Marketing Association. Back in the days when there was a lot of direct mail, when you used to get lots and lots of stuff in the mail, and even today on the late night infomercials, these people are all members. American Express is a member. Bank of America is a member. Geico, that insurance company that has ads with a lizard,

---

a gecko. And that insurance company, Aflac, that has ads with a duck. Ronco, that sells those plastic gadgets for the kitchen.

One of the reasons this organization (the DMA) became powerful and popular was because they shared their research back and forth. Back in the days of direct mail, they would mail out *this* version with *this* headline and *that* version with *that* headline. They would see which ones sold most, and they got good at it.

Now here's the interesting datum that you will find useful –

> **"The average person who will buy will do so only after being touched seven to nine times."**

Now consider this – the average person that visits a website, how often do they come back?

Answer: Never.

The statistics show us that most people visit a website once and never ever return again.

THE BASIC PROBLEM NEEDING TO BE SOLVED

1. Most people who visit a website will *never* return, but

2. most people who buy have been touched *seven to nine times.*

If you have a website and someone comes, and you don't turn the visit into a conversation, then a very few might buy … but not nearly as many as would if they had seven to nine contacts.

Therefore, since Traffic-Building can take time and money, you don't really want to invest that time and money to work on Traffic until you have a conversation system in place.

LOCATION

How many have ever heard that the key to business is location, location, location? So what does that mean? It means:

- People can see you.

- Accessibility.

- Convenience.

- The *right* people can see you.

On the web, it means you have to have your corner of the Internet.

The elements of your location online are:

1. a website, and you have it hosted by some hosting company; and

2. a domain name, which is your "address" online.

Now, the domain name should be chosen with an eye to the future: That will be the third step, which is TRAFFIC.

So you have to do a little Traffic-Planning before you can set up your location. And that makes sense, because it's the same in the physical universe.

If Location, Location, Location is important in Philadelphia, then you're going to want to think carefully about the traffic in Philadelphia before you choose the location for a store on Main Street, right?

STEP ONE: "Location"

"If you take a middle-of-the-road position, you risk getting hit by traffic from both directions." — Margaret Thatcher

---

YOUR LOCATION

Your website should have a domain that is very well-reasoned and perhaps researched to be your main key phrase because it will help you down the road. For the website sitting atop your domain name I recommend Wordpress software for a number of reasons as your site-building method because:

- You stay in control. It's easy to make small modifications to a page, to add a page, to upload new pictures, and to keep a safety backup, just in case.

- Google loves Wordpress. You can do a number of things to make yourself attractive to search engines on a Wordpress-software site.

- You need to have some kind of conversation system starting right there from that location, and it's easy to set up on a Wordpress-software site.

This book describes a simple method of setting up your location online.

Your location in the physical universe might be a storefront on Main Street and you have an address like 123 Main Street.

Your location in the online universe is something like www.WoolyBullyNeckties.com and that's your address.

Your actual location is some directory upon a web hosting computer which you've rented from a web hosting company . But your visitors don't know or care about that. All they know is: go to www.WoolyBullyNeckties.com ... and there you are.

So for establishing your location online, a quick preview of what we will discuss is:

- You will examine certain "keywords" (phrases that people type into search engines), and you'll do some analysis to determine words you want included that very important domain name.

- Then you visit a company called a "registrar" and you get that domain name assigned to you.

- Then you make some arrangements for hosting your site from a company called an "Internet service provider."

- And last, you use the "Wordpress" website-creation software, to create the pages of your website.

NOTE: I need to clarify something that can easily be confused. I recommend that you DO NOT use a FREE site like on Wordpress.com or on blogger.com ... but I'm recommending that you DO use the Wordpress software on your own site, with your own domain name.

Using a free site like Wordpress.com or blogger.com is a bad idea for a couple of reasons --

1. Many people KNOW it's a free site, and that doesn't make you look very professional.

2. If somebody else is the actual owner of your site, they could change their mind, close their doors, and all of your work is gone. This actually happened to tens of thousands of people who had put up free sites on GeoCities.com.

ABOUT WORDPRESS

At CopyDragon webwriters, we have 60 or 70 sites of our own, and we maintain a couple dozen websites for clients. And every one of these websites except one very old site now uses the Wordpress site-building software.

Over the years I've built sites with over a dozen tools: hand-written html code, website tools named HotDog, Symantic, Corel, HomeSite, Dreamweaver, FrontPage, Nucleus, phpNuke, NetObjects Fusion, and more. Lots of different tools. And ...

Fact: Wordpress will give you the most bang for the buck. It gives you, the site owner, more control and you get many built-in advantages when it comes to Google.

As the site owner, you can have a backup of the whole site on your desktop computer so no matter what happens out there, you haven't lost your site. If you want to change the date of an event from the 17th to the 18th, you can go into a hidden page, log in, type just like a word processor, hit save and it's changed. That means that you're no longer tied by a golden chain to a web designer.

Furthermore, Wordpress has a wide variety of looks and feels which can be installed with a click. That means that you can choose something, with a process which I'll describe fully in this book, so that your target customer will simply LIKE your site, automatically and unconsciously.

(I'll show you a way to use your own unconscious mind to very accurately predict which of these looks and feels your target customer will automatically and unconsciously like.)

And please realize that you don't want to build your website to tickle *you*, to please *yourself*.

Instead, you want it to please that person, your target customer ... and you yourself have had this experience. You go to a website and you say, "Oh, I just kind of like this place". Usually you don't think why. You go to others and you think, "Yuck".

It's unconscious. It's not thought-out, but you as the builder of your website can choose things that will cause the desired effect upon your target customer, just by thinking it through in the right order. That method will follow in this book.

Now, before I show you how you send people to your website, let's talk about conversation systems.

STEP TWO: "CONVERSATION"

"Consider well what you say. Talk is cheap because supply exceeds demand." — *Anonymous*

CONVERSATION SYSTEMS

Growing up in Henrietta, Texas, I had a friend whose name was Donny Burkman. I knew him when we were in first grade. I graduated with him from high school. He lived just up the block from me for many years.

Later, Donny Burkman went to work for Neiman Marcus in Dallas, Texas. Neiman Marcus is a very smart department store, very good at marketing.

Let me ask you – Have you ever gone into a store and someone came up and said, "Can I help you?"

I'll bet you have had that experience.

And what is the answer everyone gives to "Can I help you?"

NO THANKS

"No Thanks," is the answer to "Can I help you?" nearly every time. So if you want to start a conversation, do you wish to go up to your customer and say, "Can I help you?"

Not really, because the answer is no and that's the end of the conversation.

THE NEIMAN-MARCUS CONVERSATION SYSTEM

Here's what Neiman-Marcus taught Donny to do ...

The customer is walking around looking at stuff. That's what they do in department stores. As soon as they look at some object for more than a moment, you go up and say, "That's an interesting thing. Would that look good in your home?"

If they say yes, are you in a conversation?

If they say no, are you still in a conversation?

Either way, you have engaged the customer into a conversation.

And that's a conversation *system*.

Now that other phrase – "Can I help you?" – if that's a system, it's a real bad one.

LET'S MAKE UP A CONVERSATION SYSTEM

Let's pretend we're running the Neckties R Us store on Main Street in Des Moines. Not much business, so I'm standing in the doorway. There goes a woman. There goes a guy. Someone comes in. I ask them: "Can I help you?" They leave. No conversation system.

So let's make up a conversation system for Neckties R Us on Main Street in Des Moines. A guy walks by. I say: "Hello mister. That's a really ugly necktie you got. I can help you."

You're going to start a conversation. You're better off than if he just walks by and you don't say anything, right? Wouldn't insulting him and maybe hooking his interest be a better system than just letting him walk away?

Or for the woman walking by, perhaps I'll say: "Madam, I bet someone in your family is having a birthday soon. Maybe they would like a necktie."

Those are probably not very good conversation systems, and you can probably find some better ones.

For example, inside the store might say, "You know, mister, that necktie you're looking at, that's really good with the color of your skin. It's going to bring out the color of your eyes. Are you looking for something for social events, or more for business?"

Bingo. You're in a conversation.

A CONVERSATION SYSTEM IN THE ONLINE UNIVERSE

There's more than one way to build a conversation system online. But I'll describe a very common one ...

Let's imagine we got a guy and he has heard for the first time – I'm just going to pick a random subject: Tantra Yoga – he just heard of this for the first time.

"Tantra Yoga, oh that sounds kind of good," he says, "I don't know. It sounds kind of metaphysical, maybe something about sex maybe, I don't know. I like the sound of it, but I don't know. I'll see if there's any around here."

So he looks up "tantra yoga Des Moines." And he finds two websites.

1) The first one is from Dakini Amrita Stringbeany.
2) The second one is not an actual tantra practitioner at all but a masseuse of questionable authenticity, and her site is called Maya Smith's Tantric Massage. She actually has nothing whatsoever to do with tantra yoga, but she uses the phrase all over her site to give her site credibility, and she operates in Des Moines, so she shows up in the search page on Google because Google doesn't know any better.

Now he goes to Dakini Stringbeany's site. And right there it says, "Would you like to have a book that reveals the seven secrets of tantra to attain bliss and greater intimacy with those you love?"

He says, "Well, yes. I would. How do I get it? Hmm. Just put my email address here. OK!"

He clicks submit.

The next thing he knows, he gets an email. It's about the book. It says, "Hi. Thank you so much for signing up. I'm going to send your book in a minute but, you know, I hate spam as much as you do. I want to make sure it's really you that asked for this. So just click this link so I know you really want it and I'll send it right to you."

He says, "She's kind of like me. She hates spam!"

Right now, how many touches do we have?

Three? That's right. One is that he visited the website. Two is his interaction with the form, and three is the email he received.

Also, he already knows more about this woman. She hates spam. And she responds. He knows these two new things about her.

And the point is – that it's now more than one contact. He hasn't gone away. That's what most people do who go to a website. They visit once and then go away, forever. Never come back.

AN EXAMPLE: AMAZON

Now on Amazon, you would go back. Why?

One reason is that when you deal with Amazon, they deliver what they said they would, when they said they would, and they even come back to you later and suggest new things for you to buy and these suggestions are often right on.

That's why you don't go to Amazon once and leave forever. They engage you in a conversation because they have a conversation system.

DAKINI STRINGBEANY'S CONVERSATION SYSTEM

Dakini Amrita Stringbeany has a conversation system. Now, our boy, let's say his name is Dorfus Doofus. His email is DorfusDoofus@gmail.com. So he says, "Well, I'm going to confirm that I want that book."

He clicks the confirmation link.

Next thing you know, here comes an email with the book. She not only responds, and she hates spam. She's like him, and she keeps her promise and gives him a free gift!

He says, "Wow, that's great." He starts reading it. Now he's listening to her voice. That's another touch. He's learning something. This is a benefit. He has got a benefit. Here's someone touching his life, and if it's a good match, it's touching near his heart.

A couple of days later, he gets another email from her. It says, "I just wanted to let you know that I'm so grateful that you're reading the book. I want you to know that if you have any questions, you can call me. Here's my phone number".

His eyes open wide. "Whoa," he says, "the girl gave me her number!"

You might want to give visitors your phone number. You might not. But that's another way to get another contact.

Maybe he calls her. Maybe he doesn't. But a couple of days later, he gets another email. "Oh, I know her," he says, "It's that Dakini girl."

So he opens it up and it says, "We're giving a talk at the Bongo Bongo room about five ways to kiss to delight your sweetheart. So bring your sweetheart, or if you don't have one, you will learn some handy information to help you get one".

He says, "Wow, that's right down the street at the Bongo Bongo room. I could go down there and learn some of this Tantra Yoga stuff!"

So it goes ... on and on and on.

This is a conversation system. You're starting with one little thing but now it's a conversation.

OTHER KINDS OF CONVERSATION SYSTEMS

You can use Facebook for a conversation system. My friend Lisa, a Tantra Yoga practitioner in Reno, Nevada, first told me about how she gets most of her business by using a conversation system on Facebook.

What other kinds of conversation systems have you seen used online?

- One is a bulletin board, a system where people can interact, or online forum.

- Other social network sites, like MySpace, Lifestyle Lounge, and many others.

- Meetup, which is sometimes online and sometimes physical meetings.

- A blog which elicits comments and conversation with visitors.

I'm not saying that email has to be the only system – it's just the most popular one. It's not the only possible system. The point is only that it's a conversation system.

Now, let's go back to Maya Smith's Tantric Massage. Remember, this is the other site that our boy found when he was searching for Tantra Yoga in Des Moines. She's not really a Tantra Yoga practitioner at all; her website just uses these words to make her services seem exotic and perhaps a bit more respectable.

That is, Maya Smith is simply a masseuse in Des Moines, and on her site are pictures of her wearing a revealing diaphanous gown from India. Well now, if this is a very revealing picture, of course the guy might call her up. He's a guy.

But there has been no conversation. Her site presents a list of her massage services, her fees, and a bunch of revealing photographs. That's it. There's no conversation. Assuming that both sites are generally attractive to him, which person is he more likely to interact with?

If later he is to decide to buy Tantra Yoga training, sessions, counseling, or coaching, who is he more likely to feel comfortable dealing with?

Most likely, he'll feel the most comfortable with the one he "knows," and with whom he's been carrying on a conversation. He will simply feel more at ease, and will be more likely to buy from somebody he knows, likes, and trusts.

So in your own case, the simple moral is this – If you start a conversation with your website visitors, more people are going to stay in communication. And more people are going to buy.

STEP THREE: "TRAFFIC"

"Prediction can be difficult, especially about the future." — *Albert Einstein*

BUILDING TRAFFIC TO YOUR WEBSITE

There are two ways to get traffic, visitors to your site. Many people overlook the first one:

1. Send them there. You *send* people to your website.

2. Get Google and other search engines to send searchers to your website.

Have you ever given a talk? Did you send them to your website?

Probably you did. You don't have to rely on anybody. You don't need no Google. You can send them there yourself.

Now, here's something I've sometimes overlooked when I've given talks. Sometimes, I didn't give them a **reason** for going to my website. Sure, I told them the website. But not WHY they should go there. I didn't spell out the *benefit* awaiting them there.

For example, I can tell you about my website: http://CopyDragon.com. But do you know that when you go to this website all you have to do is put in your email and you will get a 17-lesson online marketing course?

So when you give a talk, give them a *reason* for going to your website as well as the website address. Sell them on going to your website. Arrange so there's something in it for them, when they go.

SENDING PEOPLE TO YOUR WEBSITE

For starters, your domain name should be on every piece of paper you have, such as business cards, brochures, any Yellow Page ads, radio ads, cash register receipts, the credit-card notation that appears on their statement, your store window if you have a physical store, anything and everything you have. Every communication line you have should contain your website address, and try to give a reason for someone to go there.

I have a therapy site. Would you like to know more about how the unconscious mind works? How it is created? How you can begin to start a conversation with your own unconscious mind simply and easily?

You can have a free 85-page ebook that explains it all. Just go to http://www.BeingHappyToday.com.

GET GOOGLE AND SEARCH ENGINES TO SEND PEOPLE TO YOUR SITE

The second way of building traffic is getting search engines to send people to you.

There are all kinds of gimmicks and geegaws and real systems and phony systems out there telling truth and lies about this, and how it can best be done. This is a big subject but here are the basics –

Matt Cutts is a PR guy for Google and he's the one that this information comes from. He says that sixty percent of Google's rating comes from this:

BACKLINKS

If I have a website and I can get other sites out there on the Internet to link to my site, then Google becomes convinced that I must be important, because so many other folks are linking to me.

In other words, Google is less impressed by how important I say I am and more impressed whenever other people indicate they think I'm important; And Google figures that if a lot of people are linking to me, then that fact says that a lot of people think I'm important.

These links from other sites to my sites are called my "backlinks."

QUALITY OF BACKLINKS

Raw number of backlinks isn't enough. For example, if that fellow over there is running a porn site, and that other fellow over yonder is running a get-rich-quick scheme, their linking to my site may even hurt me. For me to get good credit, any sites linking to me should be **respectable** sites.

And those sites linking to me should be in **harmony** with my site. If there's a barbecue pit website and it's linking to my copywriting site, there's no harmony. I'll get more mileage from some other copywriting site, or something related (book publishing, etc) when they link to me.

The best kind of sites for backlinks have **authority**. They are considered important sites; and they're generally large sites. For example, get yourself on Wikipedia if you can. Get yourself on Amazon if you can. Get yourself on YouTube – *anyone* can get on YouTube with a backlink to his own site – and that's good because YouTube is an authority site, a big site, an important site.

Make sure the page where your backlink appears is about the same **subject** as the page on your site being linked to.

In other words, if I can get a link from a site and the page their link is on is talking about the secrets of good copywriting, or how to find a skillful copywriter, or why you want a copywriter creating the content on your website, and then their link points to some page on my site where I'm talking about copywriting ... that's harmonious. And so it counts for more in the eyes of Google.

ANCHOR TEXT

It also matters what actual words they put inside the link itself.

How many times have you made a link that said "click here?" That's where they're supposed to click for information about raising mushrooms for fun and profit. Well, because the words in the link only said "click here" then Google gains no information about what you are about, because the only information in the link itself was the two words "click here."

More useful would be where the words used in the link itself are descriptive of your website or the page on your website.

The words inside the link are called the "anchor text." And "click here" as anchor text isn't very useful because it misses out on an opportunity to tell Google about what the target site's about.

For example, let us say that you are a hypnotherapist. If you can get that person out there to put a link on their site where the live words are "Hypnotherapy Des Moines" as the anchor text, that's telling Google that your site is about Hypnotherapy and about Des Moines.

Google uses this information. This is one of the ways you help Google to clearly understand what your site is about, and that's important, so that Google lists you in the right place!

So number of backlinks, their quality, the authority of the referring site, the relatedness or the harmony of the page on the referring site and the page on your site, and the actual words used in the link … these are the things that Google uses to determine about 60% of your "score," and your score with Google determines whether Google wants to put you on page one, or page forty-seven.

How can You Get Backlinks?

Now how can you get backlinks? How can you create them?

Well, you could ask people for them – and you should – but there's other ways that are better, faster, and easier.

You can write articles and put them in article directories. You can put press releases out on the Internet. You can find blogs that are related to your subject and comment on a post there, with a link (that YOU created) back to your own website.

For example, if someone has a blog that accepts comments, you'll notice it says something like "Leave a comment." Later I'll tell you how to find those kind of sites, so you can add a comment, and include a link back to your own site. Their blog post is on a subject related to your site. You go there and create a comment with a link.

Presto! A related backlink!

If you sign up with a forum, you can create a "forum signature," which will appear below every post you make on the forum. On most forums, you can create one or more backlinks in your forum signature. Every time you post something in the forum, there's a backlink to your website.

You can tweet.

You can Facebook.

You can do Linked-In.

There's more. There are things called RSS directories. This a techy name for a site which pulls content from all over the web and makes it available for other people to plug into their own websites. So you can put backlinks in some content and send it in to a RSS Directory.

There are a lot of ways you can create backlinks to your own site. There will be a list of many of these described in more detail in following pages and in the free companion video series, but the point here is to remember that you want the words in the anchor text, the actual words in the link, to be the key phrase that you're interested in Google associating with YOUR website.

In general you want about half of the links coming in to go to your main site like CopyDragon.com but not all. Some should point at pages *inside* your main site.

For example, I want some of my inbound links to be pointing at CopyDragon.com ebook writing samples page. I want the anchor text of the link out there to say something like "ebook writing samples," and I also want something like "ebook writing samples" to be the title on that page of my website.

There are a number of things you can do *inside* your site, which has mainly to do with Google understanding what your site is about.

I'll provide quite a bit of step-by-step information in the following chapters about how to get backlinks because it's a big subject. They're not hard to do but they're either going to take time or you're going to hire someone to do it.

AN EXAMPLE

I did a site for a guy that's doing helicopter tours, and he wanted to bring up his website in a hurry because there's a certain season for that business and he had just opened this business in our little area around Mount Shasta.

In two months we had 20 to 30 key phrases on the front page of Google. I built his site from scratch, did the email-capture thing, and Google was already sending searchers to his site. The number of people who have signed up on his list is growing every day, and they're receiving helpful information and targeted marketing messages as our emails follow up, so we're creating more "contacts" as we go. For his site we used a lot of these techniques and I'll spell that out in the information following.

It does take time. If you just do the first two steps – Location and Conversation – well, it's only part of the journey. You now have a wonderfully functioning website, but to which very few people are coming.

Does it make sense why the three steps are in the order I describe? Location first, then setting up a Conversation system, then setting up systems that create Traffic?

GETTING GOOGLE TO SEND SEARCHERS TO YOU

There are two ways to getting traffic to your website: sending people there yourself, and getting Google to send people.

Google is about "searching," so you want to think about what people might be searching for.

For example, the very best domain name you could have would be a domain name which exactly duplicates the most important key phrase you can think of.

Ideally, this would be the best phrase you can think of that people would type, and then Google would remember your site, and would consider you important, so Google would serve you up on page one.

Of course, it needs to be a phrase where you can do a better job of convincing Google that you're important than *all those other folks*.

So for example, you might like to be at the top of Google for the phrase: "insurance."

Oops. You're not going to get it.

Because there's whole villages of people working for Aflac and Geico and State Farm, keeping *them* on the front page of Google. You're just not going to be able to beat them out.

You might like to get automobiles, or cars. Probably not going to get first page of Google for those terms either. There's too many people already there, working for Ford and Chrysler and Nissan, defending that mountain which they already hold.

But if you're a Tantra Yoga practitioner, you could get probably "tantra yoga Des Moines." If you only operate in one location and it's Des Moines, do you want to spend your time with people from New York? Probably not. Better to spend time with people from Des Moines. So a domain like www.TantraYogaDesMoines.com might be a good thing.

Now, the exact science of picking the very best key phrases is beyond the scope of a book of this size. This subject is something we could discuss for days and days and days. And it's an inexact science, where much is unknown. Google is real closed-mouthed about what they think is important.

But we know, from Matt Cutts the Google PR guy, that 60 percent of what Google chooses has to do with backlinks that point into your site ... and 10 percent has to do with how fast your site loads.

Realize that here we're not so much talking about how *important* Google thinks you are. It's what Google thinks you are *about* when it comes to that key phrase.

For example, I'll bet anyone reading this today could go and get the domain www.RubberChickensBoulderCreekCalifornia.com right now ... but that wouldn't help your business now, would it?

Neither would GetBlissRightNow.com because no one is searching for that ... or if they are, they may have a completely different idea in mind about what they're looking for. They might be searching for religion, or Tantra Yoga, or some meditation method, or illicit drugs, or brainwave apparatus. It could be almost anything, and the odds are not good that they were searching for what you offer, even if you're delivering bliss day after day.

I won't go into how to choose a desirable physical location for a physical business, but the short and sweet approach to finding a favorable location on the Internet is going to be finding the best domain name, then hiring a hosting company where you can put up a website, and I'll later explain why a Wordpress software website has a natural advantage over almost any other kind.

LOCATION: HOW TO ANALYZE KEYWORDS

"How to judge a book: (1) Examine the cover; (2) disregard the cover; (3) read the book." — Traditional Wisdom

---

Let's take a look at keyword analysis.

Now frankly, at www.CopyDragon.com, when we are setting up sites and doing work for our clients, we use a much more elaborate and focused way of setting up keywords. Unfortunately, that subject is real big. We use seven or eight different approaches to look at this, and each one of those might be more complicated than what can reasonably be explained in this book.

What we're going to do here is to give a fairly simple method that works pretty good. It's not the ultimate way. It's not the totally best way for a professional, but it's a good way for a do-it-yourselfer, and it will put you in better shape than 98 percent of the people doing their own work across the nation and around the world.

If you want to handle this in the best possible way, then you'll need to become a professional, or hire a professional. To develop the skills – and invest in the paid tools – that a professional possesses takes a lot of time. If you are currently wanting to promote your existing or soon-to-be-created business – now – that's probably not a good use of your time. It's no more sensible than learning sign painting so you can paint a professional sign over your storefront.

So for the very best results, you can hire a professional ... but if your budget demands, you can follow the method given here, which will beat out 98 percent of the do-it-yourselfers in the world.

YOUR FIRST STEP TO ESTABLISHING A WEBSITE
To establish your site requires four things –

- Analysis (very similar to choosing the best address for a physical business)

- Obtaining your domain name from a "Registrar" company

- Obtaining site hosting service from an ISP (Internet Service Provider) company

- Site-building, using some method for creating the pages of your website, such as Wordpress software

THE BEST "ADDRESS" REQUIRES ANALYSIS
Online, your "address" (location) is your domain name.

Before you can host or build your site you need that domain name. And because your domain name can have a large effect on how Google responds to your site, you're best advised to do this analysis before choosing a domain name.

Analysis means looking forward to see what words would best serve you for your domain name, and that means looking forward to consider the future traffic to your website.

Even though BUILDING traffic is the third and last step of the Three-Step Marketing method, we must CONSIDER traffic as our very first practical action before we can do the first step of the Three-Step Marketing formula.

As mentioned earlier, the two approaches of creating traffic to your site are:

1. You will send people there yourself. That is, you'll print the domain name on your business cards, brochures, and all advertising, paint it on your store window, announce it in any radio ads, and give out flyers with your web address at any seminars or talks you give.

   AND/OR

2. You will persuade search-engines like Google to tell searchers about you, and thus Google and other search engines will send people to your website.

So, before we get into the mechanics of how to obtain your domain name, before we get into hiring webspace, and before we consider how to build the pages of your website, let's consider how we plan to relate to the search engines.

SEARCH ENGINES

Some years ago, there was a battle among the search engines. The question was: Who was to become the most popular and dominant search engine?

The contestants included names like Alta Vista, Ask Jeeves, Yahoo, Microsoft (MSN), and a few others. Then Google showed up. The others had a lot of stuff on the front page. Google had only a simple search box.

After the dust settled, Google won.

That is, they won the war among the "official" search engines. Now only Yahoo, and Bing (Microsoft renamed) remain among the top "official" search engines.

However, what many people overlook is that new classes of search engines have evolved. We just don't normally realize that they are search engines. For example –

- YouTube is a huge search engine, with a vast number of searches done every day.

- Facebook is a huge search engine, and actually has more traffic than Google, as of March 2010.

- Amazon is a very large search engine, the fifth-largest in the world, and many people search for information on Amazon, for they want a book rather than a website as their information source. (Three million searches each day)

- eHow and Yahoo answers can be important search engines, with thousands of people searching for information daily.

Later, when we consider how to build traffic, we may wish to consider how to place ourselves nicely on these additional search engines. But for right now, let's start with Google, because if you rank nicely on Google, then you'll generally also rank nicely with the other "official" search engines: Yahoo, and Bing.

Google is the best known, the most used, and the greatest number of our competitors will be found there. Google also offers the most information for our use, so we'll concentrate there.

EXAMINING A GOOGLE LISTING

Examining what's shown in a single Google listing will tell us useful information. After all, this is what *Google* thinks is important to show to us, and so conversely Google is pointing out to us what is important to Google!

Here's an example Google listing. Notice that there are three parts:

CopyDragon webwriters – copywriting services / marketing design [1]

copydragon.com   [2]

Want customers? More income? Even a local business can boost business using Internet methods, copywriting services, and automatic online selling systems.   [3]

[1] The first part is the **Page Title**. Google may show the home page for the site, or Google may show some other page on the site. In either case, this is the "title" of the page being shown.

[2] This is the **Domain Name**. If Google is showing some page other than the home page, then the **Page Name** (a filename) will be shown as well. For example:

Copydragon.com/how-to-get-customers.html

Sometimes there are folders or directories involved, so a page name may show directory information as well. For example:

Copydragon.com/downloads/free-special-report-download.html

[3] This is the **Description**. If you've set up your site properly using Wordpress software as I'll describe later, you can control what this says. Otherwise, Google may simply take the first words on the page. Sometimes that works OK, and other times it totally sucks. Because this is what the searcher sees; this is your "sales copy" to persuade the searcher that you've got what he wants!

FOUR TYPES OF DOMAIN NAME

We'll find it easiest to choose an appropriate domain name, if we examine the four possible pathways. Here are four example domain names –

Meaningless (domain is neither a brand name nor a search phrase)

Bliss All Over The Place

blissykissy.net
Some kind of store, some kind of merchandise, and some people who work there, probably in a city somewhere, it's all so dreadfully cute!

Brand Name (one my sites, where I manufacture musical instruments)

Mobius Megatar :: Guitar Lessons and Electric Guitar, Easy, How ...

megatar.com
Mobius Megatar touch-style electric bass for two-handed

tapping with fingers on strings to play bass and guitar simultaneously with piano-like technique.

Search Phrase ("plr" means "private label rights," searched often by online marketers)

PLR Article Warehouse

plr-article-warehouse.com
Whoah! "Why the Texas Wild Man is Giving Away Five Truckloads of Steer-Wrestling, No-Holds-Barred, Profit-Whomping Books and Videos and MP3s about ...

Search Phrase + Location (a site done for a client, offering helicopter tours in our specific area)

Lake Shasta Alpine Helicopter Tours

lakeshastaalpinehelicoptertours.com
Lake Shasta Helicopter tours of Shasta Lake (Lake Shasta) in Northern California for houseboat, camping, hiking and biking, water sports, Redding California.

Now in these examples, I've given the entire Google listing, but realize that, as we consider domain names, we're really only concerned with the domain name, so here's the same information stripped down ...

Meaningless   (neither brand name nor search phrase)

blissykissy.net

Brand Name

megatar.com

Search Phrase ("plr" is a search phrase used by online marketers)

plr-article-warehouse.com

Search Phrase + Location   ("helicopter tours" + "Lake Shasta") lakeshastaalpinehelicoptertours.com

These are the four paths available to you in your choice of a domain name, your "location" on the Internet.

If you use one of the paths which contains a phrase that people are already searching for, then Google will be more able to help you create traffic to your website.

If you do not use one of the paths which contains a search phrase, then Google will be much less able to help you create traffic to your website.

I cannot find any reason to recommend the first pathway. I believe people just thoughtlessly dream up some domain name they think is cute, and then choose that, without any consideration of how the choice will affect their future. (And their results? Often lousy.)

YOUR BUSINESS NAME

I've read that the choice of your business name is one of the most important decisions you'll ever make. Most of you reading these words have probably already made that choice, but just for discussion, here's what I think are useful things to have in a business name –

1) The business should say what it is, or what it does. For example, Apple Computers, or Camel Cigarettes, or Ford Motor Company. (It should not say something cute like "Western Eclectic" or "NoogyBoogie" because who knows what that means?) The worst offenders seem to be hair salons, which often use puns like "The Mane Attraction," or "Curl Up Comfy." Yes, these are clever, but it doesn't say what it is, so a person searching for that kind of thing may not even recognize them in the search results!

2) The business name should be brandable. Like "Apple Computers," not "Bargain Computers," because "bargain" is just a common adjective and it isn't very easy to create an

identity using common words. "Bob Jones Used Cars" is better than "Good Used Cars."

3) If possible, the business name should imply a promise or contain a desirable quality. For example, "Dragons Teeth Wood Rasps" and "Sony Walkman" and "Pepsi Cola" and "Costco" and "Playboy Magazine" and "Excalibur Custom Auto Shop" and "Yahoo Search Engine."

I mention the business name because it has some similarities with the domain name. And in fact sometimes it may work that your domain name could be your business name.

CHOOSING A PATHWAY
The pathway you choose will determine how much work you'll have to do when it's time to get customers to come to your site.

"BRAND NAME" DOMAINS
If you choose to build up your "Brand Name," then it may be that Google will not be able to help you as much. Here are some examples ...

"Bob Jones Insurance Company" – http://bobjonesinsurance.com – this won't help you find any new customers through Google. Yes, people search for "insurance" but what they'll see on Google page one is Geico and Aflac and State Farm. If they search for "Bob Jones" they *may* find it, but there are lots of folks out there in the news and in business who have the same name.. Of course, if they search for "Bob Jones Insurance" they'll be almost certain to find it ... but now you are talking about people who *already know* about Bob Jones Insurance. These are not searchers for insurance in Bob's town. So in this case, Google isn't helping Bob to find any new customers who don't already know about Bob Jones Insurance.

However, it's an "OK" brand name domain. It's not a great brand name domain, because the name is very weak from the point of view of branding. For example, there could easily be a half dozen Bob Jones Insurance companies around the country.

"Mobius Megatar touchstyle basses" – http://megatar.com – this is one of my sites, and Google couldn't help me much in the early years because people were not already searching for "megatar." Now, after a lot of work on my part, they do search for "megatar" and more importantly, when they search for my better-known competitor, they find ... our site! But this is because I used advanced methods and successfully associated the word "megatar" with my often-searched competitor's brand name in the mind of Google ... and it took over a year of work to do it!

However, it's a good brand name domain.

"Source School of Tantra Yoga" – http://sourcetantra.com – this is my teacher's tantra yoga school. Google cannot help very much to gather new clients. Although "tantra" and "tantra yoga" is often searched for, there are quite a few practitioners, books, and other schools on the first page. With a lot of work, perhaps this site could beat out all the others, but it would be *a lot* of work.

However, it's quite a good brand name domain.

So these "Brand Name" domains are great for claiming the brand-name online, and they're great for permitting people who already know you to find you easily when they search with your business name. But Google won't be sending you any new business from folks who don't already know your name.

"SEARCH-PHRASE" DOMAINS

The logic behind this kind of domain is that you choose your domain name based upon a phrase that people are already searching for. Here are some examples –

"Two-Handed Tapping" – http://twohandedtapping.info – this is a domain that I set up as a secondary site for my special guitars. The playing technique that allows a musician to play my specialty guitars as if playing a guitar and a bass at the same time is called "two-handed tapping." In addition, this phrase describes a particular method of playing regular guitar which was popularized by the well-known guitarist Eddy Van Halen, and others.

So there are plenty of musicians searching for this phrase every day. And when they do, then my twohandedtapping.info site comes up on the first page of Google. Now this site does have useful information for those musicians, and it also runs a set of banner ads at the top, and a number of these ads send site visitors to my main guitar site.

"Learn Conversational Hypnosis" – http://learnconversationalhypnosis.org – this is a site with a salespage which sells a training course for people who would like to learn hypnosis techniques that can be applied in an ordinary conversation.

Research showed me that quite a few people searched for "conversational hypnosis" and quite a few searched for "learn hypnosis." And some people searched for "learn conversational hypnosis." It was quite difficult to get good ranking for the first two phrases, but the third was possible, and for quite some time, searchers could find this site easily. However, this is a very competitive field, and since that time, a number of other sites have done lots of work on their traffic, and because our main business moved elsewhere, we have done absolutely zero follow up work on traffic, so as of today, our site no longer appears on the first page of Google. Although this was initially a good "search phrase" domain name, this illustrates that maintaining a position on Google can require ongoing work on creating traffic, and ongoing work to keep Google convinced of your site's importance. The good news is that this ongoing work is a lot less work than the initial work done when first establishing your website.

"Simply Free Article Spinner" – http://simply-free-article-spinner.com – this is one of my sites. An "article spinner" is a method of taking a short article, and coding it in a certain way so that from this single article can be created any number of similar articles which use different wording. In other words, they'll all have the same subject, but the words inside will be different. We'll discuss articles, and how you can use very short articles to create traffic to your website later, when we discuss how to build traffic.

But among all the professional web-building firms and online marketing folks, using such software called an "article spinner" is a fast way to create from a handful to hundreds of articles which can be used in building traffic to some website.

I wrote (programmed) some article spinning software which can be offered as an online service for anyone wanting to use this method of creating traffic. And this is the site where people sign up to use this free online "article spinner."

The domain name of this website was chosen from search phrases that people were already using: "article spinner" and "free article spinner."

As a result, for many years, a Google search on either of these phrases will nearly always pop up my website on the first page.

A Reminder

Please remember that choosing a search phrase as your domain name is usually not enough to get on the first page of Google for any valuable search phrase. Usually it takes other steps done later. We'll discuss these other steps when we discuss how to build traffic to your site.

But many people overlook the fact that selecting a properly-evaluated search phrase as the basis of their domain name is a very powerful first step that can greatly increase your later results with Google.

And because so many people overlook this simple and powerful first step, this means that *you* can take advantage of this powerful first step, and from there on, you have an advantage.

Now remember that we have to (a) think up and research an advantageous domain name before we can do the important steps of (b) obtaining the domain name, (c) obtaining web hosting, and (d) building our website itself.

That's why we're discussing the kinds of domain names first.

In the videos that accompany this book, you can watch me go through the process of researching a "search phrase" domain name, registering it, getting web hosting, and setting up the Wordpress software and creating the actual pages of a website.

You as the purchaser of this book may have free access to our membership site where these demonstration how-to videos are provided. See the Resource section of this book which tells you how to access the book site and the instructional videos.

"GOOD" SEARCH-PHRASES VERSUS "WORTHLESS" SEARCH-PHRASES

We will go over specifics later, but here's a fact to consider: Not all Search-Phrases are Equal. Because some are very useful for you, and some are not. Without getting into much complexity, here are two important considerations ...

1) **Value versus Competition.** The single-word search-phrase "insurance" is very, very valuable. After all, who wouldn't like to appear on the first page of Google for everyone in the world who's searching for "insurance?"

    But because it is so valuable to companies in this industry, they've already put a lot of work into getting well positioned, and they have entire teams of people who continue to work on staying well positioned every day ... and as a practical matter, you as an individual will not have the power and ability to beat them out on the first page.

    Similarly, other short search terms which extremely high

numbers of searches every day include "cars," "golf," "weight-loss," "drugstore," "dating," etc.

Even longer multiple-word search phrases in popular fields may have huge numbers of competitors. For example: "get a girlfriend."

So as we look for a "useful" search phrase, it must have *enough* people searching that they can create an income stream for you if/when you get on the first page of Google, but the search phrase must not have *too many* people searching or you're pretty much guaranteed to be fighting a very large number of competitors, and those competitors who are stronger, better financed, and who got there first will probably prevent your success at getting your own site on the first page of Google.

2) **"Buying" phrases versus "Freebie-Seeker" phrases:**
Given the right number of searchers – not too many, and not too few – there is also a quantitative difference among searchers.

For example, some searchers are ready to buy. Other folks just want free stuff and never intend to buy anything. And the search phrases they type into Google will often reflect this difference.

For example, "purchase car insurance" has been typed in by a buyer. And "free song downloads" has been typed in by a non-buyer.

And "barbeque" could be typed in by either someone wanting to purchase a barbecue pit, or someone wanting free recipes.

Now, in some cases, you may have a plan to attract folks

with something free, but then you think you can change them into buyers. Sometimes this works. Sometimes it doesn't. Be careful, and don't leap into getting a search-phrase domain that will appeal to freebie-seekers unless you have a *plan* to convert them into buyers!

"SEARCH-PHRASE" PLUS "LOCATION" DOMAINS

In many cases, for a local business which mainly sells to customers in a certain area, I recommend "Phrase plus Location" domains.

When you properly combine a search-phrase plus a location-name, then you can show up on searches that people often make to find somebody *near them* who has what they want.

For example, somebody who's just moved to Cleveland might search for "hardware store Cleveland." Or "car wash Cleveland." Or "attorney Cleveland," "probate attorney Cleveland," "business attorney Cleveland," "real-estate broker Cleveland," "dentist Cleveland," "insurance agent Cleveland," "Ford dealership Cleveland," and such things.

Under normal circumstances, a do-it-yourself website builder wouldn't have the ghost of a chance of appearing on Google's first page for "hardware," or "car wash," or "attorney," or "real-estate broker," or "dentist," or "insurance agent," or "Ford dealership."

However, in many cases you *may* be able to be well-positioned when you use a search-phrase plus your location. Here's a working example –

"Lake Shasta Helicopter" – http://lakeshastaalpinehelicoptertours.com – this is one of my clients, and after some research, I discovered that there are relatively few people searching for helicopter tours. However, some do, and furthermore, there is more than one service that my client offers. For example, he offers helicopter tours around Lake Shasta. He offers helicopter tours over Mount Shasta. He offers helicopter weddings. He offers helicopter discovery flights. (This is an introductory flight for somebody who thinks they might like to learn how to fly a helicopter.)

So in this case, we looked at the number of competitors who have search phrases in their names, and discovered that helicopter tours in Hawaii, New York, and other favorite vacation destinations had nice positioning with search-term plus location keywords. So we did the same thing. We chose the most useful single phrase for the domain name, and then did some additional research and work, and within a couple of months we were ranking on page one of Google results for 20-30 different search terms, all of which bring him people who are interested in some kind of helicopter flight.

(In a later part of this book, we'll discuss how to turn these one-time visitors into an ongoing conversation so that more of them will in fact choose to buy what's being offered.)

When considering a "phrase plus location" for your domain name, you still consider the numbers of searchers. It should be not too many and not too few. But remember that, if you sell a local service, then even a small number of searchers in YOUR area who are searching can turn into significant income, if they find you, and if your conversation system engages them to go into communication with you so that you can present your offer compellingly.

MANY FACTORS TO CHOOSING OPTIMAL SEARCH PHRASES

While a professional will use special tools for evaluating search phrases, and will consider a wide number of methods, you as a do-it-yourselfer can use a few simple tools, and this will generally allow you to accomplish a workable result.

You won't beat out the professionals in your field, but you can certainly beat out 98% of the other do-it-yourselfers who don't have access to the focused and workable information given in this book.

HOW TO BEGIN?

Basically, the questions of "brand name versus key phrase" and what domain name to choose has to be solved first. Because your domain name will be your LOCATION on the Internet, and what you choose will have a huge effect upon the results you'll obtain when it comes to creating new income using online methods.

What you'll be doing is this:

1) You'll think up some "Likely Suspects" keywords.

2) You'll do some research to see how many people are searching, and along the way you can also learn more about how many other people think those keywords are valuable.

3) As you research, you will uncover other keywords to consider, and you'll then run *those* keywords through the researching process, too.

4) As you narrow in on what's likely to be your best choice, you will then also check to see whether a domain name based upon that keyphrase is available, and this process may also uncover additional possibilities.

5) By means of this process, you will select what you think is your best shot, and you will then be able to go on to the next step, which is to *obtain* that domain name for your use, by buying that domain name from a company called a "registrar."

6) Once you have your domain name, you can move on to hiring web hosting service, and then to creating the pages of your actual website.

[I illustrate this entire process with the free how-to videos that are available to any purchaser of this book. Please see the Resource section in this book which tells how to access the free membership site where the videos are available for your use.]

So what's the first thing you do to begin the process of selecting a domain name?

You start with answering the question, "What are the keywords that I would like to use?" The first place you start is your own intuition for the "likely suspects."

START WITH "LIKELY SUSPECTS" KEYWORDS

For our example, which is shown in detail in the videos, I'm going to create a website that has to do with a book or a course. I haven't created this book or course yet, but it will be about "How to Create a Facebook Fan Page," for people who want to use Facebook as a conversation/enlistment system to generate income for their business or product.

Here's how I came to choose this subject for an upcoming product:

- Facebook has apparently won the social marketing war. Just a few years ago, I would say MySpace was ahead. You could put up information about yourself and chat with your friends and all that stuff. Facebook came from behind and seems to have taken over.

- As of the time of this writing, Facebook has more than 800 million active users, and more than half of them log onto Facebook on any given day. And it's still growing.

- In March of 2010, for the first time, Facebook had more traffic than Google, so realize that Facebook is a huge search engine, just as YouTube is also a large search engine.

So given that I want to create a book or course about how a business can use Facebook to find new clients, and to stay in touch with the existing client base, then the first place we're going to start is, "What are the likely suspects?"

We're going to just think them up and in this case, I'm going to say, "Well, one of the likely suspects is going to be 'Facebook fan page' and another is 'Facebook for business.'"

Now, as it happens – as you'll see from the videos – by means of researching these "likely suspects" we came to uncover many other possibilities, and in actual fact, a completely different keyword phrase appeared which checked out as being better for our use.

That final keyword phrase was "how to create a Facebook business page," and in the videos you'll see exactly the steps I took for the research that uncovered this rather-good key phrase. (In the videos, you'll also see how I checked to discover that this long phrase was available as a domain name, and how I registered the domain name, and how we set up the website-hosting account, and how we created pages there.)

For the example, I didn't use any of our advanced (paid) tools here at CopyDragon webwriters, so you can follow the same method that I show in the videos. And here in the book I'll describe the process in general, and introduce you to the tools you can use to research keywords and make a sensible choice for a domain name.

PROFESSIONAL TOOLS VERSUS DO-IT-YOURSELF TOOLS
Now if you were going to do keyword research A LOT, then I suggest you immediately invest in a special keyword-analysis tool. Get either "Micro Niche Finder" (simpler to use) or "Market Samurai" (more options).

These are listed in the Resource section of this book, and they're worth the money ... BUT ONLY IF you're going to be doing this frequently.

However, if you're simply wanting to do keyword analysis for your business, because you wish to begin creating more income using the Internet, then you should be able to get the job done using some free tools. Google provides several of them.

Let's look at some of these tools we'll be using, and then we'll go through our example.

GOOGLE SEARCH

Of course you know about Google search.

- We'll be using Google Search to see competitors listed in the search results.

- We'll also be paying attention to the number of paid ads.

- We'll also use an optional feature available on the left column, called "related searches."

- We'll also use any suggestions that appear in a drop-down box as we type the key word.

- And we'll install a plug-in for Firefox that will give us some additional information ...

SEOQUAKE

On Google, as you know, you can search for things, but I want to gain just a little bit more information, and so I've installed a free tool called SeoQuake. It's a plugin for Firefox, and Chrome and Opera browsers. (A "plugin" is a mini-program that can be easily added ["plugged in"] to a larger program; that is, the SeoQuake mini-program can be added to your browser program.)

See the Resource section of this book to get SeoQuake

Once installed, an additional line of information will appear below each website that Google Search displays, and we'll use some of this information to help us evaluate keywords.

In addition to the information described in our videos, you may wish to use the additional research features built into SeoQuake.

GOOGLE KEYWORD TOOL

(See Resource section of this book for address.)

This is a special tool that is available to you. It helps you find additional related keywords, and tells how many people worldwide are searching for various keywords.

I use the Google AdWords Keyword Tool. If you don't have an AdWords account, and you probably don't if you're starting out, Google has a similar tool called the "External Keyword Tool."

To find it, you can simply do a search for "external keyword tool."

Either version of the Google keyword tool will enable you to learn about the keywords being used on some competitor's website, and can tell you lots about any keyword or key phrase you choose.

GOOGLE INSIGHTS FOR SEARCH
(See Resource section of this book for address.)

This gives you additional information that doesn't appear under normal search. The Google Insights website provides a graph that shows how many people have been searching for a specific term over a number of years, so you can see if the key phrase is becoming more popular. You can see seasonal ups and downs, and quite a bit more.

It tells you what countries most searches come from. It provides additional related searches, and calls your attention to related phrases which have very recently increased a lot in search volume. (These are called "breakouts.")

KEYWORD ANALYSIS: AN EXAMPLE
See the accompanying videos for a detailed description of the example, because you can *see* how to go about it, step by step. The description given here is a summary of the process.

For my example, I've started by entering my likely suspect key phrase "Facebook fan page" into Google's ordinary search function (without quotes), and here's what happened ...

PAID ADS

Notice the paid ads on the right. We're going to disregard *what* they say. What's important is that there are *a lot* of them, because that tells us we have a popular term. Those people paying for ads wouldn't keep paying if it wasn't working for them.

These are also paid ads at the top of the page, with a kind of faint orange color, so the real search information starts below that. The *real* search results are called "organic search results."

Now if we search for "Facebook fan page" we'll discover that the first four organic results are from Facebook itself. We're not going to displace Facebook itself, so we begin our serious analysis *after* the Facebook pages listed by Google.

PAGE RANK

Our SeoQuake plugin gives us some information underneath each item. One of the information items is "PR" which means "page rank." It's not nearly as important as some people think, but it does give you an idea of the relative importance of a page compared to other pages on the same Google results page.

Nine is the biggest page rank number. Websites like YouTube, Wikipedia, and Facebook generally get the number nine and other numbers above five.

Ordinary humans, we don't. We'll get a page rank number of zero to about five, tops. (But that won't stop us from appearing on page one of the Google results.)

As of today when I'm writing this book, when we skip over Facebook's listings, then we come to the first search result that's not on Facebook itself.

Google displays the title "Facebook fan page" but it's really on www.SocialMediaPathways.com. They have a page rank of three.

Next comes www.SocialMediaExaminer.com and they've got a page rank of zero. Now that's interesting, specifically because it is rather low. But remember, this is the rank of this particular *page*, not necessarily the *site*. There are other things more important to Google for choosing what it's going to show here on this first page of results than page rank. But page rank is something simple you can understand to get an idea about the relative importance of the pages we see displayed.

Next in the results list I see a site named Mashable.com. Now you notice that Mashable.com has used the exact phrase "Facebook fan page" but on all the later listings, further down in the search results, we have variations on the phrase, such as the words occurring in different order, etc. (This suggests to me that if we use the exact phrase, we may be able to rank above these other folks; because it's saying that Google didn't find any other important pages that had the exact phrase.)

On checking my other "likely suspect" phrase, which was "Facebook for business," I find very similar results.

Again, there were some paid ads, and again the first four organic search terms are pages on the actual Facebook site, and these vary in page rank: four, eight, four, nine.

Then we find that same site, www.SocialMediaExaminer.com, and some other sites listed.

WHAT'S IN A SEARCH RESULT?
There are three parts to each search result that Google displays. Here's a made-up example, for how I want my new website to appear –

How to Create Facebook Business Page
howtocreatefacebookbusinesspage.com
If you're considering how to create Facebook business page, then you're onto today's best method to find new customers, make your existing customers think even ...

So if I do a search for "Facebook business page" then Google will display it with the key phrase bolded –

How to Create **Facebook Business Page**
*howtocreate**facebookbusinesspage**.com*
If you're considering how to create **Facebook business page**, then you're on today's best method to find new customers, make your existing customers think even ...

Knowing what I want to see for my own website, I have a clue to see where the competing websites now being displayed may be weak.

Again, remember that Google uses other factors to determine who it displays on the front page ... but ... we might as well start with a strong thing that we CAN arrange, so that we begin the job with an initial advantage. And having a domain name, a Page Name, and the Description containing the exact search phrase is a good advantage.

Since we must have a domain name in order to build a site, we might as well start with the smartest, most powerful domain name that we can, right?

UNCOVERING THE BEST KEY PHRASE
You will go back and forth between the three tools:

1) Google Search

2) Google Insights

3) Google Adwords Keyword Tool

In the Google Search, you will enable (from "advanced search options" in the left column) the "Related Searches" feature. You will also notice what appears in the dropdown box when you are typing in a search phrase.

In the Google Insights, notice the "related phrases" near bottom of page, and "breakout" phrases near bottom of page.

In the Google Adwords Keyword Tool, pop in a web address for a site that's already positioned nicely on Google results, and ask Google Adwords to show you the keywords related to *that* website. Note any additional key phrases that might be revealed by the Adwords Keyword Tool.

In the Google Adwords Keyword Tool, pop in your desired key phrase and analyze how many global searches that keyword has. You can click on "Global Searches" and the keyword tool will organize the long list of keywords from Largest to Smallest.

LOOK FOR THESE SIX THINGS:

1. Find a key phrase that optimally has 4000 global searches but no more than 16000. This is no guarantee that you can get page one, because other factors are actually more important to Google. But it *tends* to indicate a pretty good phrase.

   If you can't find one in this range, then take one with a range from 2000 to 20000 global searches per month. (Note: If your Google Insights told you that nearly all the searches were from the Philippines, and you're selling into English-speaking countries, then use the Local Searches numbers instead; there will often be less local searches than global searches.)

   If you can't find one in the range 2000-20000, then try to find one with 1000 to 22000 searches per month.

   If you can't find one in that range ... uh, keep looking, if you can.

2. You want to see some sites on the Google search first page that have non-exact phrases being displayed. Because you have a better chance of bumping folks that don't have the exact search phrase in their domain, page name, and description.

3. You'd like to see non-important sites listed on page one of Google. Ie: lower page rank, and/or clumsy descriptions and page naming.

4. You'd like to find sites that don't have a lot of existing "backlinks" coming into them. Although I didn't describe this in the how-to videos, there's a button on the Seo Quake listing that shows Yahoo's count of existing backlinks. (Yahoo is better for reporting backlinks than Google is.)

   The number and quality of existing backlinks into a website is actually the single most important factor Google uses to determine a site's "importance," so if you can find competitors who have done this poorly – ie: who have relatively few inbound backlinks – then the more easily you can bump them down and appear above them.

   We will discuss backlinks *a lot* in the "How to Get Traffic" section of this book, so I'll not discuss it very much now.

5. Use the CPC ("Cost Per Click") information from Google Adwords Keyword Tool to guide you toward selecting a phrase which is at the same time valuable, and yet not over-the-top competitive, and consider the presence of some paid ads to indicate desirable phrases on Google Search.

6. Avoid using "Freebie-Seeker-Attracting" search phrases in favor of "Buyer-Attracting" search phrases, though sometimes this will not be an issue.

BACK AND FORTH. ROUND AND ROUND.

Go back and forth between these tools, and go round and round … and along the way, you'll usually find a search phrase which has enough, but not too many searches, and you can *probably* use this as the basis for your domain name.

Remember that if you use the "Phrase plus Location" type of domain name instead of simply a "Search-Phrase" type of domain name then you don't need to have as many people searching, because they're all in your neighborhood, and you're more likely to get them into your shop because they were searching by your location.

Remember that **in many cases, I recommend the "Phrase plus Location" approach**, especially if you're planning to use a high-value search term like "auto insurance" or "cosmetic dentist" because you *may* be able to rank on page one for "auto insurance Topeka" or "cosmetic dentist Topeka."

Keep notes as you go, about the phrase you find, and for those of possible interest also note the number of searches and CPC number as a rough indication of how much traffic that search phrase is already experiencing.

CAN YOU GET THE DOMAIN?

There are a number of sites here and there that give you information about what domains are available. In the early internet before webpages, you could uncover the owner of a site by using the command "whois." And so a website giving information about who owns a domain has come to be called a "whois" site. For our purpose here, my favorite is called "Psychic Whois," and my reason is that when you use Psychic Whois, it gives you LOTS of additional good ideas about related phrases.

These new ideas can then be carried back to your research with Google Search, related searches, Google Insights, and Google Adwords Keyword Tool.

For our discussion here, let's assume that you have found a term which seems good, and which gets a reasonable number of searches. Comparing what shows up now on Google results, you suspect you can get your site onto Google page one.

In the example shown in detail in the videos, I have found howtocreatefacebookbusinesspage.com. And now I need to see whether it's available as a domain name.

So I go to http://psychicwhois.com.

I can type in "howtocreatefacebookbusinesspage" or I can type in "how to create facebook business page" and psychic whois will show me both the availability of the specific domain I'm inquiring about ... and also, as you type the inquiry, psychic whois will suggest other possibilities.

Once you've found the domain you want, I suggest that you do *not* register your domain through Psychic Whois. You can get better deals elsewhere.

LOCATION: HOW TO SET UP YOUR DOMAIN NAME

"You will make a name for yourself. Think carefully what it might be." — *Terrence Trumble*

ENOM

I'm going over here to my favorite registrar which is called "eNom." In the box for "search for domain," I'm going to enter:

HowtoCreateFacebookBusinessPage.com

Sure enough, eNom says it's available. Good!

Now eNom is going to try to sell me some additional domains which I don't want, so I'm going to unclick these other domain versions. I'm unclicking the *.co version and unclicking the *.net version, and unclicking the box for the *.org versions. I only want *.com.

The reason that I like eNom best is that some of the others, like GoDaddy and NameCheap, make you go through a long series of pages where they seemingly attempt to trick you into buying additional services. I don't want additional services, and GoDaddy and NameCheap annoy me and waste my time with the long series of pages they present.

But eNom makes this one attempt to sell me a few additional variations of the domain, and then that's the end of it. So after making sure I've only got the *.com box checked, then I can go to my cart. I already have an account, and I've logged in, so I can simply confirm that I'm buying it, and it's done.

NEW ACCOUNT

Of course, if this is your first time to eNom, you'll need to set up an account. They'll ask your name and address and credit-card number. They offer a couple of ways to pay them. I usually just keep a credit in my account.

They will also ask you to set up some information for the public "whois" information. There are actually four records, but you can simply do the first one and tell them the other three are the same.

(Remember, the "whois" information is the official online record of your name and address as the owner of this domain – as in "who is the owner of this domain?" – and this information is normally a public record that's easy to find on the web.)

AVOIDING SPAM

A couple of years ago, an extensive experiment led to a report on how spammers create the lists to which they send their spam. Well over 90% of their lists are made up from emails they find posted on websites. So if you put a naked email address on any website – a forum signature, a post, your blog, your website – then expect the spammer's robot program to find that email address, and then expect your email box to crammed with spam for many years.

And one website the spammers especially like is the "whois" information that can be publicly obtained online. It's a public record. So there are two things you can do to minimize this hassle –

1) Create a phony persona for these public records. Go ahead and use your ordinary snail mail address, because this doesn't seem to create snail mail spam. But set up a name you can recognize, and a different email address. I use "Reg Smith" so I know that any email I get addressed to "Reg" is spam extracted from my registrar's public whois information. (The registrar itself will communicate with me through my *account* email, not this public "whois" email.) And you set up a separate email address, which you can then filter out in your email client. Mail for Reg? Toss it!

2) Some registrars offer a "hide your whois" information feature. If this is free, you might want to do it. But if it costs I'd recommend just using an identifiable name and separate email so you can trash the incoming spam. Your choice.

So after you've set up your account and purchased your domain, now you are the "owner" of that domain.

However, anybody going to that domain will just arrive at a default page there at the registrar, because the registrar doesn't know yet where your website is!

UPDATING YOUR 'NAME SERVERS'

Now this next step can only be done *after* you have set up web-hosting with an Internet Service Provider (ISP) company. But I'll describe it here because it's the next step and the final step to be done on your registrar account.

So as to make this comprehensible, let's look at how the Internet works.

THE INTERNET IS A TELEPHONE SYSTEM

The Internet was a variation of the normal telephone system, and it's actually still a telephone system. It works very similarly to the telephone system you know.

You pick up the telephone receiver on your desk and you open up a phonebook and you look up Joe Smith and his number is 818-522-5207. So you dial that number. It goes through to the telephone set attached at that number, and you hear Joe Smith pick up and he says "hello."

The web works very much the same way. When you type the name of a website into your browser, then the browser on your computer acts as if it's going to dial a number, but it's a number on the internet rather than a number on the regular telephone system.

Now in this case, there is something like a phone book computer already on the Internet, and your browser can actually look up the name, and get the number. This "Internet phone book" computer is called a "Domain Name Server."

That just means it looks up a domain name, and hands out the Internet "phone number." An Internet "phone number" looks a little different from an ordinary phone number. An Internet "phone number" looks like this – 225.168.2.38

There are four numbers separated by dots. Now this isn't the number of a telephone located in some city. Rather it is the number to reach a website located on a website-serving computer, somewhere, in some country. The domain name is called a URL, which means "Uniform Resource Locator." And that just means it's the "name" for some specific address (Internet phone number) on the web.

And the number with the dots in it is called an "IP address," which just means "Internet Protocol" address, very much like 123 Main Street is an address on a street downtown for the hardware store, and (530) 938-1100 is the number for the telephone in my office.

Now when you type a "name" (domain name) into your browser, and your browser fetches the actual number for you (the 123.22.168.7), you don't hear Joe answer saying "hello," because what happens is that your browser actually is sending a request for a file, called a web page.

The answering computer, the web-server computer, then sends out the file called a web page, and your browser uses information in the file to display the web page all pretty for you. (The browser will have also requested the pictures specified in the file, so they're also displayed on the page in the proper places.)

DOMAIN NAME SERVERS (DNS)
The point is that there are these computers already out there on the Internet which act like a phone book, translating what you've

typed ('www.copydragon.com") into some number (like 78.22.0.127), so that your browser can request and receive a file and display a webpage for you.

Now because we use a uniform address system on the Internet, (the URL and IP-address) then as you might imagine, the Domain Name Server computer also has a URL (domain name) and an IP-address. And we don't have to think about the IP-address, but we will want to know the URL (domain name) for the DNS Server that serves *our* website.

When you have hired website-hosting service from an Internet Service Provider company, in the email they'll send you, they will include the domain-name of the DNS. They will actually send you two domain names. They will look something like this:

> ns1.bonkytonky.com
> ns2. bonkytonky.com

TELL YOUR REGISTRAR YOUR DNS NUMBERS
The one thing remaining that the registrar needs is to know what these two DNS numbers are. So after you've purchased your domain name, go to "my domains" and find the domain you've just purchased and click on its name.

You'll then be offered several choices and one of them is "DNS Servers."

On the DNS Servers page, unclick the "our servers" radio button, and do click the "custom servers" radio button.

You'll then type in the two DNS server names and save the page. You'll probably get a warning that you'll be losing the whiz-bang valuable services the registrar provides you but that's just fine. Because you don't want your visitors going to the registrar's site ... you want your visitors to go to *your* site, and only your DNS servers know how to get your visitors to get onto your website at the web-hosting company.

Once you have saved this information, then the registrar company will broadcast what you've told them to all the "Internet phone books" (DNS servers) around the Internet. This can take from five minutes to three days.

You'll know when it's complete, because when you use your browser to go to your domain, you'll no longer go to the default page at the registrar's. Although there may not be much to see there just yet, you'll now go to your new website instead!

That's all there is to it!

LOCATION: HOW TO SET UP YOUR HOSTING SERVICE

"To rule a country, one must act with care, as when frying the smallest fish." — Tao Te Ching

---

So now that you've purchased a domain name from a registrar, you'll need to purchase website hosting from an ISP (Internet Service Provider) company.

In the Resource section, you will find one or more links to some recommended site hosting Internet service providers. They will offer various services; what's important to you is that they offer:

- "cPanel" (a back door that allows you to set up classy email accounts, like arthur@copydragon.com instead of arthur127@gmail.com)

- "Wordpress" (or "Fantastico" which allows you to quickly and easily install Wordpress)

When you sign up, they will send you an email that has some information on it.

This email will show your domain name, your user name, and a passcode. This email will tell you the names of your two DNS servers.

The email will also show you a link where you access this backdoor called cPanel (and that just means *control panel)*. "cPanel" is a brand. There is more than one type of control panel that these servers have, but cPanel is frequently used and I recommend it. It's helpful to have a control panel. It makes it easier for a non-techy person to operate the server.

What happens is that you go to a certain back-door address that they will have given you, and you will log in with your username and your passcode and you'll be looking at cPanel. Watch the demonstration videos to see what it looks like.

HANDY AREAS IN CPANEL

CPanel has several handy areas. We won't cover them here, because you can access tutorials about cPanel if you want to. But the areas that might be of interest are –

- You can change your password

- You can set up email accounts that look professional: arthur@copydragon.com

- You can do file transfers (FTP). Occasionally this is useful, but FileZilla (a free program which runs on your computer) is better

- In cPanel, you can use something called Webalyzer to see how many people visited

- You can use something called Fantastico to install Wordpress

So let's go to Fantastico. Fantastico will install a number of different things which might or might not be useful but 99 percent of the time, we're only going to use it to install Wordpress.

The people at the ISP you've hired may be willing to install Wordpress for you. And then they'll give you the special back door address for Wordpress, and how to log in. So you might not have to do this step of installing Wordpress yourself. But if you do …

So I click on Fantastico, and then I click on Wordpress.

> Please watch the free demonstration videos to see the exact steps to enter cPanel, choose Fantastico, and install Wordpress.

STEPS TO SET UP WORDPRESS USING FANTASTICO

We're going to choose new installation and we leave "what directory" blank which means that it will install Wordpress right on your domain.

It will ask you for the "admin name." You could type A-D-M-I-N but that is a bad idea. That's a traditional administrator username, but hackers are going to be looking for a username A-D-M-I-N. So don't use that.

So make up a username that you can remember but which will be hard for anyone to guess. I like to use combinations of letters and numbers that have meaning for me.

For example, let's say that I had a girlfriend named Mary and that was 1965 and her last name was Martin, Mary Martin in 1965. I might type Mar65Mar.

To make it weirder, I could go Mar65_Mar and that's going to be really hard for anyone to guess, but pretty easy for me to remember.

Similarly, I like to use a similar scheme for a password. So if I live at 55 Sutter Street, in San Francisco, I might choose something like suTT55_SFran. Easy for me to remember; hard for anyone to guess.

Next I enter the email where I want to get any email that this website sends me. Not email that somebody visiting the website sends, but if Wordpress itself needs to let me know about something.

Enter our site name: How to Create Facebook Business Page.

We want some kind of a slogan next. The label says "description" but it's really a slogan, or positioning statement. I'll type in "Using Facebook to Increase Income."

Then I click the "install Wordpress" button.

Now for some reason, Fantastico does half of the install, and then wants you to click again to finish the installation.

In this example, and in the demonstration video, I'm installing via Fantastico. There are other ways you can install Wordpress, and you could find tutorials or hire somebody to help you, but Fantastico is the easiest one I know. It's usually available on any server that has cPanel.

So now it just finishes the installation and then it tells me some computer gobbledygook about where the site is located.

If you want it to send you an email with details about the installation, just in case you need the info, you could put your own email into a box and it will send an email with those details.

Presto. Wordpress is now installed.

LOCATION: HOW TO SET UP WORDPRESS

"The future never just happens. It is created." — Will Durant

---

ABOUT WEB-DESIGN

Please bear in mind, at CopyDragon Webwriters, when we provide a done-for-you service for a client, we use Wordpress nearly all the time.

Over many years, I've used over a dozen different methods of building websites, and generally speaking these years of experience have taught me that Wordpress is the easiest, fastest, best-looking, and most Google-happy method you can use.

In addition, the non-techy owner can manage Wordpress easily after it's built, can make backups, change a date on a page, write and post an article or a picture, and more.

Because of this approach, CopyDragon webwriters can *always* provide a website that works better for making money than a typical website created by a "web designer," and usually our approach costs only a fraction of a web-designer's fee.

Now don't get me wrong. There are some exceptions to this but your typical web designer is usually a graphics person who wants to make something that's real pretty, and real pretty isn't necessarily what sells.

WHAT APPROACH MAKES YOU MONEY?

I remember a story about Howard Johnson's. That's a chain of restaurants across the nation. Back in the 50s, they were everywhere, and the Howard Johnson's company was having a problem because people stayed in the restaurant too darn long.

The restaurants were all along most highways, and the restaurant would make the most money if they could bring the people in, feed them and get them out of there.

But people were staying around and around and around and around. Dawdling. Spending hours at the table.

Finally someone figured it out. It was the paint. The paint and the décor was real pretty, and very relaxing. They'd created a very soothing and relaxing restaurant. So no wonder that weary travelers were taking time to relax and rest up.

What did the Howard Johnson people do? They changed the paint to bright orange and other loud colors that clashed a bit. To this day, if you can find a Howard Johnson's, you will find that they have this orange color because they discovered this important fact:

*What made them the best business was **not** what was real pretty.*

And it's the same for you. Sure, it's great if your website looks attractive.

But wait a minute … attractive to *who*?

You?

Nope.

Attractive to your *customer.*

So if I'm selling to teenage boys who want to play a violent, gothic video game, my website will NOT be something that pleases me … instead it must please and attract those teenage boys who like violent, gothic looking things.

And the problem with web-designers in general, is that they only focus on what looks "real pretty" or really flashy, and they try to please *you.*

And what your client finds attractive, and what will actually speak to your visitor to get them to engage in a conversation and spend money ... that's something else.

And that something else – actually creating an income machine – that's what we do for clients at CopyDragon webwriters.

And ... that approach is what I'll be sharing with you in this book.

THEMES – THE LOOK AND FEEL OF YOUR WEBSITE
Wordpress is website-creating software.

It doesn't sit on your computer; rather it sits on your website and offers you a back door where you tell it things it needs to know. And from what you've told it, Wordpress creates the pages of your website for your visitors to see.

Wordpress was originally built as blogging software. But it evolved, so that now we can use it for a regular website. It doesn't have to be a blog, although it could *contain* a blog, or it could easily *contain* a page with articles or news.

Wordpress is designed with a focus on ease of use, elegance, and performance, with a huge selection of themes and plugins. Themes make it *look* different. Plugins make it *act* different.

LET'S EXAMINE THE WEBSITE
Let's go look at the website. If we've done our job right, we should be able to see it now at:

www.HowtoCreateFacebookBusinessPage.com

By golly, there it is!

At present the look and feel is set by the default theme. Remember, themes let you choose how your Wordpress website *looks*, and plugins are little bits of code that you can stick in there that change how it *acts*.

We can see the name we gave our Wordpress site, and our slogan.

This fresh Wordpress installation first appears all set up as if you were going to use it for a blog. (A blog usually has the latest articles, also called posts, on the home page; A "normal" website usually has a welcome-page or salespage for the home page.)

We're going to change your Wordpress website to have a more normal home page. The default Wordpress first appears with a sample blog post with a sample comment, and one sample page.

Now, just as there is a backdoor that lets you access cPanel, the Wordpress software has a backdoor and you will access it like this:

  www.yourdomainname.com/wp-admin/

Here you use that admin username and password to log in, and then you'll see the "Dashboard."

BACK DOOR AND FRONT DOOR

I find that the easiest way to work inside Wordpress is to open the backdoor in one tab, and the front door in a different tab.

Since I'm looking at the backdoor "Dashboard" right now, I'll just hold down the control key and then click on the site name at the top of the page, which is a direct link to the site as a visitor sees it. That "front door" view will now open in a new tab.

For our done-for-you clients at CopyDragon, we set up all these things, and the client doesn't have to worry about all these choices in the left-hand column. After we've set it up for the client, the client only has to learn three things:

1) How to change some words on an existing page, like change a date, for example.

2) How to upload a picture.

3) How to stick in a new article or some news.

Then, everything updates automatically.

But if you're setting up your own, we'll here go over the most essential things to get you going.

CHOOSE AND SET UP A THEME

The first choice you must make is to find and install a theme, so that your website will have a particular "Look and Feel" that will automatically and unconsciously appeal to your visitor.

Now this may sound difficult, but there's a way to go about it, which is pretty easy for most people.

We'll be making use of a problem-solving part of the mind that you use all the time, but maybe not very consciously. We're going to use your unconscious mind to solve this problem, and most people will actually find this very easy to do. And the solution that comes up will generally work very, very well.

This step can be a little tedious, but let me explain how it works.

Your conscious mind is logical, and very good at excluding things it deems unimportant, and in many cases that will mean it excludes "feelings" and "hunches."

Your unconscious mind is not very logical, and it's working all the time, handling things that you have either shoved into the background of your focus (like how to tie your shoe) or things that you can't really explain. For example, if you jump off a diving board and do a somersault before entering the water, that's done with the unconscious mind, because the conscious mind can't really think that fast. So, background stuff like riding a bicycle, tricky body learning, and vague stuff like feelings and hunches and intuitions, all that is the unconscious mind at work.

(If you'd like to know a *lot* more about your own unconscious mind, how it was created, and how you can get into better communication with your own unconscious mind for greater happiness and better problem-solving, just request the free book

"How to Find Happiness in an Unhappy World" at
http://beinghappytoday.com.)

Since you are not your customer, and yet you wish to select a
theme that appeals to your customer rather than you, how do you
solve this problem?

Easy.

You go and look at themes, one at a time. Picture your typical
customer. If you're not sure about your typical customer, go back
and review the Happy-Life formula section early in the book.

And for every one of the themes you look at, simply ask yourself,
"Does my customer like this look?" The answer may be a feeling
rather than words, but you'll know.

You may know *why* it's true, or you may not know why it's true,
but trust your intuitive knowledge. Your unconscious mind is very,
very good at this. Just let it work, and it will provide you with very
reliable answers.

Find 3-5 themes that you feel your target customer will like.

Choose the best one. Go with that.

Other things to guide your choice:

- Usually, it's best to have the site name at the top, and
  maybe a picture, so avoid weirdo layouts.

- Usually it's best to have a main column and one sidecolumn.

Here are good places to search for themes –

1) Wordpress.Org (choose 'extend', then 'themes' and preview
   likely ones)
   Benefit: They're free.
   Downside: Most are not as well-designed as paid themes.

2) Elegant Themes

3) Woo Themes

4) Refined Theme

5) Studio Press

You will find links in the Resource section.

SETTING UP THE PAGES AND THE PARTS OF YOUR WEBSITE
Please refer to the demonstration videos for a step-by-step
demonstration.

You are going to do these things ...

Pages and Posts

Pages and posts are very similar except that pages are more or less
permanent. Posts are typically added-to frequently. Think of posts
as news or articles. You might have a new article every day, or
every week, or every month, or now and then.

But pages are part of the "permanent" structure of your website.

There's going to be some initial page the visitor sees, which you
might call a home page. You might call it a welcome page. It might
be a sales letter. But it's the one they first see.

On some of the other pages, you're probably going to tell them
something about your service and your product and maybe your
fees. Then, if you're smart, you'll have three or four pages that
Google likes to see. You make Google happy, and Google will make
you happy.

Google-Happy Pages

For example, Google likes to see a site map. That can be done very
easily in Wordpress and once it's set up, it will update
automatically whenever you make any changes.

Google likes to see a privacy page. Very easy to do in Wordpress. You can do it with just a few clicks and a complete Google-happy privacy page appears.

Google likes to see a "contact us" page.

Google likes to see a "terms and conditions" page (sometimes called "terms of service" or "terms of use").

Plug-Ins that add Functionality

You'll add some "plugins," which enable your website to do additional things. For example, one plugin will create a complete "Privacy Page" for you. Another will create a complete site map. Another will create an 'email us' form.

CREATING YOUR PAGES AND NAVIGATION BAR

Please see the demonstration videos for step-by-step information, and tutorials on using Wordpress are widely available on YouTube as well.

On the left-side of the navigation bar should be your "hello" or "welcome" page , the first page your visitor sees. On the right-side of the navigation bar should be your "contact us" page. In between, you list the other pages presenting whatever you think important for visitors to know.

You shouldn't use more than 5-6 items on the top-level navigation bar, because more than that will confuse visitors. Any additional pages need to be added *below* the top-level pages, and your theme should have provision for drop-down selections to choose these additional pages.

RECOMMENDED PLUGINS

For our clients at CopyDragon we use many plugins for this or that, but we find that we use certain plugins all the time. Here is a list of recommended plugins –

- Akismet – clears out spam comments rather well, free

- BackupBuddy – very powerful backup method, pricy.

- Dagon Design Form Mailer – very nice email-form mailer, free. (Note: some themes already have an email-form mailer built in.)

- Dagon Design Sitemap Generator – creates a sitemap page easily, free

- My Page Order – rearrange pages in the navigation-bar, free. (Note: some themes may have provision for doing this via a "menu" section.)

- Privacy Policy – automatically creates a Google-happy privacy page, free

- Simple Archive Generator – automatically creates an archive of your posts, free

- Wordpress SEO – a good plugin for customizing what Google displays, free

Frankly, there are a few more we use on nearly all sites, but some of those are our search-engine secret weapons, and others are just too complicated to explain in this book.

The free plugins can all be found on the Wordpress.org site, under "extend" and then "plugins." (Note that that is Wordpress.ORG and not Wordpress.COM which is a free-site place you should not use.) On Wordpress.org, you can use the instructions given there, tutorial videos on YouTube, or instructions on your dashboard's "plugins" section to upload them to your website and turn them on.

Please see the demonstration videos for a step-by-step demo of how these plugins are activated and set up.

The plugins above are mostly free, except for BackupBuddy. If you don't want to buy BackupBuddy, there is a backup facility built into Wordpress which is pretty good. If you ever had to recreate your site, it would recover your page content and quite a few things like that, but you'd have to redo many of your settings, contents of the sidebar column, etc.

BackupBuddy isn't cheap, but it backs up *everything* so that if your site was lost, or if you want to migrate somewhere else, you can take a complete site copy from your own computer and bingo-bango-bongo, there's your site all restored where you want it!

SETTING UP YOUR "SETTINGS"

We're only interested in a couple of these settings and again, if you have a done-for-you solution, you're never going to have to bother with these things. Someone is going to do it for you.

Under "appearance," choose "themes" to upload and activate the theme you wish to use. Notice that some themes have advanced options, and I can't really map those out here in this book because themes can vary. The advanced options may include things like the general color, setting up the menus, and quite a bit more. In the how-to videos, I used a theme with modest custom options so you can see what that's like but your theme may vary.

Under "general settings," you'll recognize the site name and description. This needs no change.

Under "plugins," activate any plugins you're going to use.

Under "settings," go to "permalinks" and choose "custom structure" and enter "/%postname%/" and save it.

Now, under "settings," go to "reading" and, assuming that you've already created the pages you want, and that perhaps you have an article or two ("posts"), you're going to change a couple of settings to make a "regular" page appear as your home page instead of the default, which is to show articles (also called blog posts) as the home page.

Now, if you don't have your pages yet, then make some. The how-to video will show you how to create and save pages.

Under "reading settings," unless you want a blog-style website that shows your most current articles on the front page – note: weak for selling! – then set the default page to be your "welcome" or "hello" or "sales" page. Then set your "articles" page to be where your "posts" will appear.

Under "settings," if you have activated the "my page order" plugin, then open its settings panel, and drag and drop the pages so your "welcome" or "hello" or "sales" page is first, and "contact us" is last. (Note: some themes use a special 'menu' section to accomplish the same thing, and in that case you needn't use the "my page order" plugin.)

Under "pages" click on your "welcome" or "hello" or "sales" page. Enter your content, and assuming that you've activated the Wordpress SEO plugin, then enter what you want Google to display for page title and description.

On each page, remove "comments," but you'll leave them on all posts. This is so visitors can comment on your posts (articles) but not on your main pages. To do this, on any page, open the "screen options" which is near the top right, and tell it you want to see "discussion" options. Once that's selected, then scroll way down, and you'll see a box to uncheck "comments." All pages and posts will now offer you the comments box to check or uncheck.

Under "appearance," choose "widgets" and here you'll drag and drop what you want to appear in the narrow sidecolumn. A "widget" is a name for a small area in the sidebar that displays something. Widgets can display different kind of things. A "text widget" will put a box in the sidebar, and any text you type into that box will appear on the sidebar of your pages. A "search box widget" will make a search box appear in the sidebar of your pages. See the demonstration videos to see how this is done.

The most useful thing to appear at the top of the sidebar would be your free offer, but you probably don't have that done yet, so you might want to drag in a text widget, and then type in some general promo about your company.

For additional widgets, I suggest dropping in a search box, and a categories box, and finally a copyrights and credits box.

ADDITIONAL "SIDEBARS"

Some themes will include more than one sidebar, sometimes a "footer," and occasionally a "top bar" into which you can drag widgets. (The term "footer" means the area at the very bottom of a web page. Much like Microsoft Word, where the "header" is what appears at page top, and the "footer" is what appears at page bottom.

If you have a footer area provided in the theme you're using, that's a great place to put things that aren't very important to selling to your visitors, but which are good for Google reasons to be there. For example, a footer area is a good place to stick in some text navigation with nice keywords inside the links, maybe place your copyright and credits down there, and maybe a "recent posts" or "recent comments" widget.

Step One of "Three-Step Marketing" is now complete!

There you go. Let's review the "Location" step of our Three-Step Marketing formula.

- We have searched for keywords.

- We have registered a domain name.

- We have rented a space on ISP for hosting.

- We have installed Wordpress and begun to fill it with content. That is step one, your corner of the Internet, your **Location** online.

Next, Step Two of our Three-Step Marketing formula will be Conversation. In other words, "How do you change a one-time visitor into an ongoing conversation and then a paying client?"

We'll turn to that next.

CONVERSATION: HOW TO CREATE A FREEBIE

"There's always free cheese in a mousetrap." — Anonymous

REVIEW: WHY A "CONVERSATION SYSTEM"?
It really boils down to this:

1) The average visitor goes to a site one time, and then NEVER returns.

2) The average buyer opens his wallet after 7-9 contacts.

Therefore, what you want to do is to engage that one-time visitor into a conversation, so that a number of contacts are created. Somewhere along the line, perhaps after 7-9 contacts, this prospect becomes a customer. He's gotten to know you, he's beginning to trust you, and he's been thinking about what you offer for a while now. He's ready to buy.

For the vast majority of people who come to your website, this would never happen, because most one-time visitors leave forever, never to return ... unless you engage them in a conversation.

And to do that?

We'll use a conversation system.

FREEBIE AND DRIP-EMAIL AS A CONVERSATION SYSTEM
There are a number of conversation systems possible, but by far the most popular one in use today is where you offer an "ethical bribe" of something that the visitor would consider to be valuable. And in return for receiving the freebie, the visitor gives you his email address.

As part of the deal, you then can communicate with him via email, sending one after another. Some of these emails will give him more free information, helpy information, perhaps entertaining information. Some of these will tell him more about yourself so he gets to know (and trust) you. Some may refer him back to your website so that he becomes more familiar with going to your site. And some may be a sales pitch.

Please see the how-to videos for a step-by-step demonstration of one simple method for creating a freebie.

A freebie which can be downloadable is your best bet, because you don't have to spend anything on printing or postage or packaging, plus the immediate-gratification makes the visitor feel good about "doing business" with you.

If you have such a conversation system, then of course you want your site visitor to be certain to SEE your offer. For this reason, you'll put it at the top of the sidebar so that it appears on every page (with a graphic picture of the free book for example) … or you'll use a pop-up form that appears when he first arrives. You may also have an inside page which makes the offer, with something like "free book" in the navigation bar.

The most valuable asset in most businesses is said to be the client list, and that's certainly true for your online operations, because this list (and permission to send emails) permits you to continue to communicate, and that ongoing communication is what changes a one-time visitor to a paying customer.

EXAMPLES OF FREEBIE OFFERS

Take a look at the following freebie offers. Notice that each offer is created to appeal to the target customer for that particular website:

- http://beinghappytoday.com – a therapy website
  Offers a free "learn about your own mind" ebook

- http://megatar.com – a specialty guitar
  Offers a free "how to play guitar" method book (ebook)

- http://lakeshastahelicopter.com – helicopter tours
  Offers a free "things to see from a helicopter" adventure travel guide (ebook)

Notice that each offer is specific to the target customer. For example, the "unconscious mind" freebie probably wouldn't appeal to the play-guitar customer. And the "how to play guitar" freebie probably wouldn't appeal to the helicopter-tour customer. And the "helicopter travel guide" freebie probably wouldn't appeal to the therapy-site customer.

Notice the minor differences in *how* the offer is presented. On the therapy website, the offer appears in a right-side column. On the guitar website, it's a pop-up window, and also there's an inside page that makes the offer. On the helicopter website, the offer appears on a left-side column.

Notice what's the same in each offer: There's an eye-catching graphic representation of the book, and then some brief sales copy, and then an email-capture form.

If you're hiring a done-for-you solution, this can all be created on your behalf. If you're doing your own, and you don't have graphics skills, you can probably hire the artwork and the 3D book cover done on an online-jobs website like Elance.com or Guru.com.

TYPES OF FREEBIES

I recommend you do not mail out something physical. It's expensive and time consuming, and if you're slow about it, it makes the guy unhappy, even when he's paying nothing!

I do recommend you use a downloadable product, or a free online service. Online service can be very good, but it requires programming skills so that you can *create* the online service. I have one online service at http://simply-free-article-spinner.com.

But generally it's easiest to offer a downloadable product, and typically there are these few kinds of downloadable products ...

1) An ebook, in Adobe "pdf" format. (If your download is too short to call an ebook, then call it a special report or even a hot-sheet or tip sheet.)

2) A recording in MP3 format. (This might be how-to information, or an interview, or a musician's song.)

3) A video (several formats possible). You could offer a download of the video or simply access to one of your (hidden) online pages where the video is streaming.

4) A list. You could offer a database in excel format of the best 25 radio stations who will interview musicians, or you could offer a written list of the seven 'best-price' wholesalers of audio equipment or travel packages, or a report about 46 sight-seeing attractions.

5) A software package. Easier than it sounds. You can buy software packages that you customize with your name, and then give them away, from companies selling "rebrand software." Sometimes quite affordable, and software can have high perceived value with your customers.

6) A get-one-free coupon for some desirable small product in your local store.

Before you go overboard with a highly-complex project, remember that a desirable freebie need not be complicated. It just needs to be seen as *valuable* and that means it can be short and simple ... just as long as your target customer would want to have it.

If you're creating a site in your existing area of expertise, then you might just start writing down the questions that people frequently ask. The answers to those questions must be valuable information, because people keep asking about it. Right? So packaging that information, in any convenient manner, could make a great freebie!

FAST WAYS TO CREATE A FREEBIE

In the demonstration video I show how you can quickly create an ebook using what is called PLR, or "private label rights" materials. If I wanted to find some PLR material on the subject of buying an auto or choosing a dentist, I can simply search for "buy a car" or "choose a dentist" plus "plr" and I'll find plenty of material I can buy, and then re-use for my ebook.

As it happens, I actually operate a website which contains over 100,000 PLR articles on all kinds of subjects, plus hundreds of PLR ebooks, so you could also simply sign up at http://plr-article-warehouse.com and most likely you'll find anything you need right there.

Here are some ways to create a freebie:

- Assemble an ebook from PLR materials as demonstrated in the companion video series that comes with this book.

- Write a freebie ebook or report using Microsoft Word. It could be how-to information, or a list of the seventeen best something or other.

- Create a discount coupon that offers some popular small product you carry for free. (This could work especially nicely if they must come into your local store to redeem it, because that creates foot traffic immediately.)

- Speak a special report using Dragon Naturally Speaking voice-recognition software. Some people have better luck with this method than other folks. It helps if you can speak steadily and clearly. The software transcribes what you've said into a text file, which will usually need a bit of editing.

- Have yourself interviewed, or you interview somebody else who's an expert on the subject. Capture the audio with a Zoom H3 device if you're interviewing face to face. Or sign up for Audio Acrobat if you wish to legally record an interview by phone. Then either offer the audio as a freebie, or transcribe it into Word and then "print" as a pdf document.

- Make a video, either a demonstration video, like "how to season a frying pan" that shows the steps. Or it could be simply another interview, but in video. Or you can use Jing or Camtasia software to capture computer screen shots. (Several of our how-to videos were created using Camtasia, which has more power than Jing.)

- If you have some understanding of web programming, think of a simple online service. You needn't program it yourself; it could be contracted out through online job exchanges like Elance.com or Guru.com. For example, it might be simple to create a special online search engine which uncovers this or that (by sending pre-formatted queries using a free Google on-your-site search box).

- Search the "rebrand software" companies to see if they're offering anything that would especially appeal to your target customer.

If creating a freebie ebook, make it look pretty by using a nice template in Word, with plenty of subheads and short paragraphs to make it easy to read. Create a title page, a table of contents, and at the end include "about the author," and links to any other products you offer, and a contact information page.

(See Resource section of this book to find software mentioned.)

SOMETHING OF GREAT VALUE

The most important thing about your freebie isn't how slick it looks. It's not how big it is, nor how elaborate.

The most important thing is whether your one-time site visitor will think, "I want it."

When it comes to information, don't be afraid of giving away the farm. Measured tests show that, if you were selling a book, and you gave away 50% or 75% of the book online, your sales would go UP and you'd make more money than if you worried and didn't give them much.

YOU ARE AN ENCYCLOPEDIA

If you are operating in a field that you know, you may not realize that you are a walking encyclopedia of information that ordinary mortals will find totally valuable.

To illustrate, imagine that you have a buddy and he's a Mercedes mechanic, and you drive a Mercedes. One afternoon, at a ball game, you ask him about the clunking noise you've been hearing. Now ... are his words golden?

You bet they are.

And in *your* field, your word are golden.

Just think about what people most often ask you about your subject, and what you usually tell them. Now write that down.

Presto. Valuable freebie.

CONVERSATION: HOW TO SET UP A DOWNLOAD

"Before I built a wall, I'd ask to know, what was I walling in or walling out?" — Robert Frost

---

OVERVIEW

There's more than one way to do this, but we'll do it like this –

- We'll create a (hidden) folder on the website

- We'll upload the freebie into that folder

- We'll create a (hidden) get-free-thingie page in Wordpress

- We'll also create a (hidden) thank-you-for-signing-up page in Wordpress

- After the guy signs up on your email form, you'll have an automatic system which adds him to a "mailing list."

- Your automatic system then sends him to your thank-you-for-signing-up page, so that he's returned to your website

- Having captured his email address, your automatic system will then send him several emails.

- The first or second of these emails will have a link to the hidden get-free-thingie page on your website where he can download the freebie

- He can then simply right-click on the link on the hidden get-free-thingie page, and save the freebie to his desktop

That's all there is to it.

UPLOADING FREEBIE TO A HIDDEN FOLDER

The easiest way to do this is to use a FTP program. FTP means "File Transfer Protocol." I recommend a free FTP program called "FileZilla" and the Resource section will tell you where to get it.

In the demonstration video I'll show you how you use FileZilla to connect to your website and then you can see the folders and files of your website.

First, you create a folder called "download" or "downloads," and then use your browser to go peek at it to make sure it's where you think it is. For example, if you've created the folder named "downloads" then in your browser you should be able to see the (empty) folder when you browse to:

http://yourdomain.com/downloads/

Next, using FTP you upload your freebie to the inside of that downloads folder.

Now, using your browser you should be able to see the freebie inside the downloads folder when you browse to:

http://yourdomain.com/downloads/

For various reasons, it's a good idea to have the name of your freebie with no spaces in it. So instead of naming your freebie "How to Win Millions at BlackJack.pdf" it's better to name it shorter with no spaces, like "WinMillionsBlackjack.pdf."

Next, copy down the complete address of your freebie, like this:

http://yourdomain.com/downloads/WinMillionsBlackjack.pdf

HIDING THE FOLDER CONTENTS

If you only have this one download, then you're set.

If you think you might have other downloads later, then you may want to make sure nobody can peek inside the folder.

The way that a web folder works is that, if there is a page named "index.html" or "index.htm" or "index.php" then that page will be offered to your browser to display.

But if there is no file with one of these names, then the folder simply displays the filenames of the files sitting there. That's what we have right now.

So if you don't want people to see what's inside that folder, then all we have to do is to create a page named "index.html" which will display, and they can't see what's in the folder. (Anyone with the correct full address can still download the freebie, of course.)

In the Resource section of this book, you have access to a simple webpage called "SilenceIsGolden-index.html" and you can use that. Download it to your computer, and then upload it into your hidden folder.

Then rename it from "SilenceIsGolden-index.html" to "index.html."

Now, if you browse to http://yourdomain.com/downloads/ you can only see this page, which says "Silence is Golden" and nothing else.

But when you later send an email to your customer that says he can get his download at:

 http://yourdomain.com/downloads/WinMillionsBlackjack.pdf
he will be able to do so.

Now you've set up the download.

CREATE TWO HIDDEN PAGES IN WORDPRESS
Go to the Wordpress back door and in the 'Pages' section, choose 'add page,' and then create a page with a title something like "Get Free Book."

Using the 'visual' tab, write the content of this page, telling how great the free book is, and how he can download it by simply right-clicking on the link below.

Add the link, using text like "Click Here to Download Book," and above the text window click on the hyperlink icon (looks like a chain link), and then paste in your download's address:

http://yourdomain.com/downloads/WinMillionsBlackjack.pdf

Assuming that you previously activated the plugin called "Exclude Pages from Navigation" then you should find, on the right hand column a checkbox with this label, and you uncheck the box, so that this newly-created page will not appear in the navigation bar.

Save the page.

Next, create another page, also which will be excluded from navigation, called something like "Thank You!" and on that page you profusely thank your visitor for requesting the freebie and you also mention that they'll be getting a confirmation email with a link they need to click, to confirm it's really them that requested the freebie.

You might also suggest on this page that they "whitelist" your email address, so that any email that comes from you won't get put into spam folders by accident.

And then at the bottom of this page you might want to create a link that takes them to some other, more useful page on your website.

Save your thank-you page.

Now you've created a get-free-thingie page, and you've created a thank-you page and both of them are hidden, in that they won't appear on the navigation bar. If you want to be thorough, then go to the sitemap plugin, and among the plugin's options you enter the page numbers of both these pages. Where do you find the page numbers? They're shown in the address bar at top of your browser when you have the page open for editing. If you do this then these pages will not be shown on your sitemap page.

You are going to need the full address of both of these new pages, so write them into a notepad file. If you set up your permalinks as instructed above, then the two addresses will be something like –

http://yourdomain.com/get-free-book/
    and
http://yourdomain.com/thank-you/

Using your browser, make sure you've got these right and that you can see the pages.

OK, your freebie is ready for downloading, and the two Wordpress pages you need are set up and ready to be used!

CONVERSATION: HOW TO SET UP YOUR MAIL MANAGER

"Don't stray far from the unbeaten path." – Paul Turan

WHY USE A PAID MAIL MANAGER SERVICE?

When it comes to sending out email, you know you can easily send out email just like you've already been doing. Perhaps you use Thunderbird or Microsoft Outlook on your computer. Or perhaps you use an online service like gmail.

Why pay money to some "Mail Manager" company just to send out email?

There are some real good reasons not to use the "free" methods you're using now. In fact, I can think of 10,000 reasons.

First, there's a law called the CAN-SPAM Act, and it sets penalties for sending out "spam," which is defined as unwanted and unauthorized emails. The penalty for sending one spam is $10,000.

If someone turns you in – even if they signed up last week – then that's a bad thing.

Even if you go through the process and beat the rap, think of the time lost.

Now, in practice, you as an individual, sending out relatively small numbers of emails, are not very likely to get busted. But given the drastic possibility, would you want that kind of exposure when it's so easy to avoid the problem?

Because when properly set up, with an opt-in confirmation email and an 'unsubscribe' link at the bottom of every email, and the full contact information required by the law at the bottom of every email, with a paid Mail Manager service if you ever have a complaint, you now have a third party, a professional company of high repute, saying, "Oh, no, this email is in complete compliance with the law. Here, our records show the recipient opted in, and confirmed the opt-in, and all emails complied fully with the law."

End of problem.

Secondly, a paid Mail Manager service will handle many things automatically much better than you ever could. For example, immediately sending out a confirmation email whenever somebody subscribes, and putting them on the list only when they confirm, satisfying the "double opt-in" requirement.

And for example, immediately removing any subscriber who clicks the "unsubscribe" link. And for example, immediately updating the information for any subscriber who clicks the "update" link.

These things might be doable on your business computer if they happened only once in a while, and if you stay near your computer round the clock every single day ... but as you grow in success, the hassle and time grows exponentially. If your time has any value at all, better to use an automated system and be free of the work, the hassle, and the mistakes.

Third, any good Mail Manager systems is quicker and faster than doing it on your computer, and gives you powers and abilities far beyond your normal email program. For example, broadcasting to your entire list ("Valentine's Day Special!") or setting up automated emails to go out to each new subscriber, for example, once every other day for as long as you like.

And of course, given this "auto-responder" system to send out what we might call "drip email," then it becomes a simple matter that any subscriber can be sent his link to download the freebie very promptly. He'll like that.

WHY NOT CHANGE OVER LATER?

If you're counting pennies, you might be tempted to think about using your computer email program "just at first" and then changing over later.

The problem is that people who have done this generally report that they lose 80% of their list trying to get folks to sign up *again,* long after the attraction of the freebie is gone, and after some of the folks have actually forgotten who you are.

It's not worth it.

If you're going to benefit from online marketing, then set up a conversation system. And the smart way to set up a freebie/email conversation is ... hire a paid Mail Manager service.

TWO EMAIL MANAGER COMPANIES

The most popular email manager company among online marketers is probably Aweber.

Now Aweber is fairly simple to use, has good features, and is well respected.

But the company I use is Auto Web Business, which is actually a private partner of the underlying company which is named 1ShoppingCart.

And the reason I use Auto Web Business is because I can have a complete shopping cart integrated with my email manager. Many of you will not need a shopping cart. For example, if you're just selling one thing, you could sell it using PayPal. So having a shopping cart may not be important at all.

However, if you *ever* think you might want to have an integrated shopping cart, then know that Aweber doesn't offer that service, and attempting to migrate your mailing list would lose a huge chunk of your list, so if you think you will *ever* need an integrated shopping cart, then simply hire Auto Web Business in the first place.

Plus, as best I can tell, Auto Web Business costs a little less.

Question: Since Auto Web Business is just a marketing partner for the "real" company, which is called 1ShoppingCart, then why not sign up with 1ShoppingCart?

You can, but if you think that you will ever be recommending a mail manager or a shopping cart to other people, then Auto Web Business has a very generous referral fee ... and 1ShoppingCart isn't nearly as good. Since you get the identical service, the identical tech support, the identical training videos and all features, it's better to go with Auto Web Business.

As of the time of this writing, the monthly fee is $29 a month. This will change when your list gets larger, as it will, but that won't happen till you have over 10,000 people on your mailing list. When you have that many, if you're doing your email marketing at all correctly, you won't care at all. You'll be happy!

Links to Auto Web Business and Aweber are given in the Resource section.

FIRST-MONTH TRIAL OFFER
Both companies offer a very cheap first month offer.

But be careful. If you sign up with Auto Web Business for the $3.95 first month, they will renew you at a full package with a shopping cart that costs $100 a month, unless you change the billing before the month runs out. Set yourself a reminder, and change to the $29 package before it renews automatically a month later, OK?

SIGN UP AND CREATE AN AUTO-RESPONDER
First you simply sign up using the "Start Now" link. You've done this kind of thing before, name, address, credit-card, etc.

After you've set up an account, then you need to log in, and under the "Email and Marketing" button, choose "autoresponders," and then "create new."

It will ask you to name the auto-responder. I prefer to use a name that tells me what the project is. So if I was capturing addresses for my "How to Create Facebook Business Page" website, I'd name the autoresponder something like "FacebookBusinessPage."

It will ask you for the return email which will display on emails which are sent out. Of course, this needs to be a valid email. You can use your general email address, or you could use your cPanel to create a new email address for this purpose. (If you create a new one, remember to set up your email reader to check in and collect any emails sent to this address.)

You're going to generally use the double-optin approach for reasons I explained earlier, and that means your customer will be receiving a confirmation email. Auto Web Business has a number of default emails you can use, and you can also set up a custom opt-in email. They will have to approve your custom opt-in email, so for right now you might want to simply choose the first opt-in template.

Inside the emails that you can write for sending out, there are various "short codes" that you can insert which will fill in with information they have on hand. For example, in the opt-in template #1 you'll see it says something like "Dear {$firstname$}," and that simply means that if Bobby Smith signed up, he'd get an email that says "Dear Bobby," which is kind of cool.

There's another code for your "signature" and this means some info that you've put in which has your business name, contact address, etc. This is something they plug in at the bottom of every email that goes out, which satisfies the CAN-SPAM requirements.

You don't have to do anything about this "signature" right now, though you might want to make a custom signature later, which includes links to your offers. Again, because of legal compliance, they must approve any custom signature, so don't worry about it now.

Once you've set up the autoresponder information, it will want you to enter a first message. This is the first message that will go out to people after they click the confirmation link on their opt-in email.

This email will need your "from" email address, and a subject, and you fill in the box with what you want it to say.

HTML VERSUS TEXT EMAILS

You can send simple text emails, or fancier ones using HTML. I recommend you start with text emails at first for three reasons –

1. Spammers use html emails a lot, so a few more of your emails will get through to the recipient when your emails are text.

2. Text emails are easier to create.

3. When you put a link like http://yourdomain.com into a text email, it gets changed into a live link automatically when the guy gets it. But when you stick a link into an html email, you have to do an extra step. If you forget the extra step, the guy will see the link, but it's not a clickable link. Bummer.

THE TWO MOST IMPORTANT PARTS OF AN EMAIL

Many emails that people receive are never opened. If they don't open them, then they can't read them. If they don't read them, then they can't be tempted to buy, right?

So it will pay you to think carefully about the two things that most make people open the emails:

1. Who it is FROM. As they get to know you, if your emails are engaging and useful, then more and more people will open them.

2. The SUBJECT should hook their interest.

I like to combine these in a format like this:

{mktg online} from Arthur – Seven Weirdo Secrets for
Fatter Sales

The first part is always the same, so that people start to recognize it, and it says in the most compact form possible, what my emails – all of them – are about. Then I may or may not say from Arthur. In general I will, because I'm wanting the recipient to get to know me as a person, and it makes the email more personal.

And the second part is a headline that hooks the interest.

WRITING COMPELLING HEADLINES

There was a fellow named John Caples, who wrote a book many years ago, called "Tested Advertising Methods." It's still one of the best books you can get about how to write an advertisement. In it, he says, "If you only had an hour of time to write an ad, spend three quarters of the hour getting the very best headline you can."

The reason is because if the headline doesn't hook them, they won't read the rest and so the rest doesn't matter. So you're better off having a darn good headline and then sales text that just sucks than having a sucky headline and wonderful sales text because with the sucky headline, no one reads the sales text. The great headline, they read it and a few people will still buy. Make sense?

Now for email, the headline that gets them to read it is of course the subject line, and people have different views about how to do it. It can be kind of a big subject but the thing is you have to get them to open the email. I'll not add detailed information here about how to write the best headlines, though in the Resource section I'll provide some additional places where you can learn more about that, including Caples's book.

THE FIRST THREE EMAILS

Here's a simple little formula for the first three emails.

1. The very first email (after they've responded to the opt-in email), is to Establish the Relationship. And one good way

to do that is to provide a gift. And since they signed up for a freebie, give them the freebie now as their gift. You will make an email that contains the address of the hidden get-free-book page you created earlier. When they click the link in the email, they'll go to the get-free-book page on your website, and on that page they find the download link. Easy!

2. The next message needs to be something personal about yourself. Useful and compelling if possible, but revealing something more about who you are. For example, the subject might say "How I Stumbled Backwards into Facebook Success" or "How a Hot Tantra Yoga Instructor Taught me about Facebook." For this one, you might want to write the story as an article on your website, and include a link in your email to send them to the article, after you've teased them with what you've written in your email.

3. The third email will fill them in on what to expect from you, and if possible give them another gift.

Please watch the demonstration videos where you can see the creation of three emails following this formula, and how you check them against Spam Assassin to make sure you're not going to trip a lot of spam filters, and how you set them up to be sent out.

How to Create an Email-Subscription Form

Now that we have an auto-responder and it has some email messages in it, let's create a form that you can put on your website that will sign people up for that email list and also for this particular auto-responder series of emails.

It's easy.

Below the "email and marketing" button, you choose "create form," and the system will lead you through the process.

It will ask whether you want an entire html page or just the form information. You only want the form information.

It will ask you what information is to be requested on the form. Email is *always* requested and is mandatory, because Auto Web Business will store all of this person's record under that email address.

I always ask for the person's name and make it "required" because I often use the {$firstname$} tag to insert their name into the email.

I do not request anything else. FACT: The more you request, the fewer people will sign up, as has been determined by many carefully-measured experiments.

It will ask you what auto-responder you want assigned, and in the drop-down box you'll see the auto-responder you just created, so select that one.

It will ask you where you want them sent after Auto Web Business has captured their information. Paste in the full web address of the thank-you page which you created earlier. It will be something like this:

   http://yourdomain.com/thank-you/

It will ask if you want Auto Web Business to "send form values by email." That means do you want to receive an email that shows you that "Joe Blow signed up for this information." You might like to know about that, at least at first.

Now it will show you a box which contains all the html code for the form.

Windows users, place your cursor inside the box, and do a Control-A which will highlight all the html code, and then do a Control-C to copy it all to the clipboard. Now you've captured the form information! (Mac user? Do your Mac thing.)

GET THE FORM ONTO YOUR WEBSITE

If you have your free book offer inside a widget in the side-column, then you'll open up that widget and paste in the form information right after your text describing the swell book.

If you have your free book offer on a particular page on your website, you'll open that page, select the "html" tab, and paste in the form information where you want it to appear.

If you have your free book offer on a pop-up form, then you'll go to settings, open up the plugin that provides the popup form, and somewhere on the settings page will be a box where you paste in the form information.

Test it from start to finish to make sure it's working the way you expect.

Bingo Bango Bongo.

Done.

Traffic: How to Search-Engine Optimize your Website

"To steal ideas from one person is plagiarism. To steal from many is research." — Throckmorton Downs

---

How Google's Business Works

Understanding what Google is trying to do will help you understand why Google focuses on certain things in the way it operates.

Google is a business. Where does their income come from?

It's not from display ads all over their front page, like you see on Yahoo, or the old Alta Vista, or the old MSN search. Because, as you will remember, Google started off with a very stark, simple front page. This immediately made them *different* from all the other search engines of the time.

Google's Income

So where does Google's income come from?

As far as I can tell, it comes from their Adwords/Adsense system.

It works like this: Once Google became dominant, they began selling little advertisements on the right-hand side and above the regular search results. If I'm a merchant and want to buy one of these ads, I go to Google "Adwords" and set up an account and place some ads. Every time some visitor to Google search clicks on my ad, I pay Google some amount of money.

Next, Google pays out money to anybody who wishes to display these ads on a private website. So if you had an appropriate website and wanted to display some ads, you could sign up for Google "Adsense" and from your Adsense account you'd get some code, place it on your web page, and some of Google's Adwords advertisements would then appear there. Then, whenever one of your site visitors clicks on one of those ads, you get paid something.

Naturally, Google collects a larger amount from its merchant buyers in the Adwords program than the amount Google pays out to its affiliates in the Adsense program.

Next, Google brings out more and more services that are free to web users – services like Gmail, Picasa, Google+, Google Docs, Google Knol, Google Images, Google Maps, Google News, and more – and guess what? These are all new places where Adwords ads can appear, making money for Google. Cool beans for Google? You bet!

GOOGLE'S NUMBER ONE RULE
Google become dominant by following one rule.

Google makes its money from Adwords-buying merchants, but who does it have to satisfy first and foremost? It has to satisfy people who are using the Google search engine.

How does Google attempt to satisfy the search engine users? By doing everything it can so that the search results yield up what the search engine user wanted to find.

And that means that Google will be *ruthless* in setting its search algorithm to disregard, and even penalize, anybody who's trying to "game the system." For example, once upon a time you could get to the top of any search engine results page just by repeating the key phrase 20-30 times in the background using white text. The visitors never saw it, but the search engines did and figured you must be the best, because the phrase was there so many times. No more. Try that, and Google will push you to page 537, or even "delist" you which means you don't get included in any search results at all.

And it also means that Google is forever tweaking and tuning its search algorithm to make it hard for people to do simple tricks to fool Google. While tricking Google might be good for *you* and your business income, our friend Google feels that your tricking the search engine users is simply a no-no.

Google doesn't tell much about how it selects the websites, and how it chooses the "most important" one ones to display first. But some of it has been revealed. Some of it has been figured out by experiments. And some of it is just common sense.

Here's what we know …

HAPPY SEARCH ENGINES: ON-SITE AND OFF-SITE

We know that Google considers some things about your site itself. But it doesn't stop there. Google also considers some things that exist "out there" on the Internet, on other folks' sites.

For example, if seventy-bazillion websites out there link to your site, then Google figures that you must be important, since so many websites out there thought you were important enough to link to you.

And if you're in the barbecue business, and all those websites out there are linking to you by using the words "barbecue" then by golly, Google figures that your site must be about barbecue. Sure, your own site said "barbecue," but when all those other sites' links say that your site is about barbecue, Google really believes it.

Now, many things on your site need to also say that you are legitimate, and important, and Google has its ideas about finding this and that which are persuasive that your site is important … and that you're about barbecue!

So to become well-ranked on Google, you need to do certain things ON your website, and you need to get certain things done OFF your website.

- The things you do ON your website have to do with the way your site and pages are written and how they are focused around your most important key phrases.

- The things you do OFF your website have to do with getting links placed out there on other folks' websites, and those links point to your website. They're called "backlinks."

GOOGLE: YOUR FOCUS

The first thing Google needs to figure out is: what is your site about?

And then, beneath that question, Google wants to know what each page is about.

So if you have a site about barbecue, for God's sake don't add pages about the cute baby clothes your wife knitted for little Janie. Because every one of those divergent pages makes it less clear to Google that you are about barbecue.

These days, the "meta keywords" are not as important as they once were – they're so easy to cheat, that Google lost all belief that meta keywords were reliable – but let's use meta keywords as an example. (Newbies, the "meta keywords" are a part of a webpage, not normally seen by the visitor, purely put there for the benefit of search engines, to tell the search engines what your page is about.)

If you were going to list the meta keywords for a page about barbecue pits, then ONLY list "barbecue pit" and then one to three other phrases which are very closely related. Don't list a hundred subjects; that clouds the focus. Use only a few, all closely related.

How to find out what is closely related? Why not use Google search, and activate the "related search" option for the search results?

So your keywords might be: "barbecue pit, barbecue pit design, barbecue pit for sale"

Do **not** make a meta-keywords list like this: "barbecue pit, great recipes, aprons for outdoor cooking, photos of 4th of July, Aunt Sally, Jack Daniels flavored potato salad, Methodist church, silly dogs, baseball game, old Ford truck."

If Google saw this second list, how would Google even begin to have a clue to know what this page is about?

Now, these days, Google doesn't pay much attention to the (hidden) meta-keywords ... but Google DOES think this way about the *visible* words on your page. And about your page title. And about the page filename. And about any tags on your photographs.

That is, Google looks at all these parts of your page, and examines the words being used, and uses this information to figure out what your page is about.

So the first thing for you to consider is that you want your entire site to be **focused**, so Google can tell **clearly** what your site is all about. And you want every page to be focused, for the same reason.

GOOGLE: YOUR IMPORTANCE

Once Google has an idea of what you're about, now Google needs to figure out how important your site is. That is, if your site is about barbecue, then ... Is your site the most important and useful site in the world about barbecue, so that Google should list your site first, before listing anybody else?

Now for my musical instrument business, which is named "Mobius Megatar," you can bet your bippy that we'll be listed first when someone searches on our business name. Because we're the most important Mobius Megatar website in the world, for certain. We even beat out Wikipedia and YouTube for "megatar" and "mobius megatar."

And that doesn't help us at all, when it comes to search marketing. Sure, if somebody searches for your (unusual) business name, you'll be first, but that didn't bring you a new customer, right? They must have already known who you were to enter that search term.

I've had local businessmen tell me with great pride that they were listed first in Google for their business name. Like for example, as of today, if you search for "Al Johnsons Swedish Restaurant," you'll find Mr. Johnson's business. It's located on Bay Shore Drive in Sister Bay, Wisconsin.

But this kind of search result means nothing when it comes to attracting new customers who have never heard your business name, because the newbies won't be searching for your business name. Now in Al Johnson's case, the good news is that if you search for "swedish restaurant Sister bay," you'll find him. So if you're travelling in Wisconsin, and want a smorgasbord, you are in luck!

What's even more important for Al Johnson ... if you simply search for "Swedish restaurant," you discover that big Al is number one on Google. Now that's some spicy Swedish meatball!

Google has determined that http://aljohnsons.com is about "Swedish restaurant," and that the website is focused, and Google has also decided that it is the most important Swedish restaurant website in the whole world. That's very good for our friend Al Johnson.

START WITH YOUR HOME PAGE

Although some people think that the "backlinks" out there in the cyber universe may be the most important thing that determines how well your site gets ranked in Google search results, it's easiest to start on your own website, because you control it.

Further, if you have 100 backlinks and a focused website, you'll probably do better than 200 backlinks if your website is not focused on a single subject.

As you'll recall, a Google search result looks like this –

How to Create **Facebook Business Page**

howtocreatefacebookbusinesspage.com
If you're considering how to create **Facebook business page**, then you're onto today's best method to find new customers, make your existing customers think even ...

In this case, the most important key phrase is "Facebook business page" and the search phrase, for which we think we can rank on page one, is the **longer** phrase "how to create Facebook business page." You'll notice that this longer phrase is also included in the Page's Title (first line), and it included in the Domain Name (second line), and in the Description (third line). That would look like this:

How to Create Facebook Business Page
howtocreatefacebookbusinesspage.com
If you're considering **how to create Facebook business page**, then you're onto today's best method to find new customers, make your existing customers think even ...

In addition to including your most important search phrase in these three places, it should also occur near the beginning of the text on the page, and near the end of the text on the page. The page should have at least 400 words. You *could* stick it into the "alt tag" for a picture if the home page has a picture. (An "alt tag" was originally for people whose browsers couldn't show pictures, and its purpose is to provide an "alternative phrase" to display instead of displaying the picture. While these phrases are rarely seen by the web visitor these days, Google always sees them.)

Want to do a little more? Stick a couple of the "related search" phrases into the text. Want even more? Try to use the keyphrase as a subhead, or bolded or italic in the text. But ... don't go overboard, or Google will see that you are "keyword stuffing," and will penalize you! Your key phrase should not occur as more than 3% of the page content. How to measure? Refer to our free Keyword Density Tool in the Resource section of this book.

NOTE: If you have installed the Wordpress SEO plugin and activated it, you will have boxes near the bottom of the screen, when you're editing the page you've selected as the home page for your Wordpress website. In those Wordpress SEO boxes, you can simply write the Page Title, and the Description. If you've chosen your domain correctly, you already have the key phrase inside your domain name.

Key-Phrases for Google

When you build a website and web pages, you're working to please two entities. One is Google, so Google will help you. So you create the architecture and some parts of the writing to please Google, by focusing the content and the titles.

Meta Description for the Humans

The description that you enter needs to please Google, but it must also be an advertisement which lures the humans to click through. After all, they'll be looking at a page of Google results. There will be other websites listed there. Some of them are probably listed before your website.

What will make those humans click through to *your* website?

The listing itself must be your advertisement. The Page Title is a Headline, and the Description is the pitch, the angle, the promise, the benefit, the attraction.

Repeating your Key-Phrase

You are going to repeat your key-phrase all through your website. Perhaps on nearly every page, and in the links inside your website that point to the other pages on your website.

Page Title –

Optimally, each page should have a title that includes the most important key phrase, or which includes a "related search" phrase. (Of course, the "contact us," "privacy policy," and "terms and conditions" pages don't need your primary key phrase; we don't normally want Google driving folks to these pages anyway.)

Now Wordpress has the habit of taking your page title and turning it into the words on the navigation bar. And so if you use long page titles, then you'll have room for only a couple of navigation-bar buttons, and it will look pretty stupid.

So here's what you do –

First, wherever possible, give your pages a one-word title. For example, at present on the CopyDragon website, we're using a top-level navigation bar with these buttons:
Hello ... Services ... Samples ... Clients ... About ... Contact

But near the bottom of every page when you edit the page, it's easy to use Wordpress SEO boxes, so that although the navigation bar stays simple and clear, the Page Titles could change like this:
CopyDragon webwriters - copywriting services / marketing design (hello)
Professional Copywriting Services | Internet Advertising Systems (services)
Business Writing Samples | Sample Websites (samples)
Commercial-Writing Testimonials, Web-Content Clients (clients)
(about: no change)
(contact: no change)

Now the navigation bar will still be clear and simple, but with the Wordpress SEO plugin you can begin focusing your site, first around your most important key phrase, and then individual pages which are focused upon related-search phrases, that is, around related topics.

Page Filename –

When we set the Wordpress "permalinks" we gained the ability to set the 'filename' of each page to be anything we wish. By default, the permalink will be created from the title you gave the page. So on our CopyDragon.com site, if we originally name the page as "Samples," then the automatically-created permalink will be:
http://copydragon.com/samples/

However, if you wish, you can change the page 'filename' simply by editing the permalink which is just under the page title on the "edit page" panel. Click the 'edit' button, change to any keyword-rich phrase you wish. But put no blanks into the permalink. Instead, separate the words with dashes. For example, the permalink might say:

http://copydragon.com/commercial-writing-samples/

Meta Description –

Just as you did for the home page, for any other significant page, you fill in the description box in the Wordpress SEO section near the bottom of the "edit page" panel. Include the keyphrase(s) to make Google happy, but write the description to entice the human who sees your page listed in the search results. Because you want that human to become entranced, and to click through!

Near Text Beginning –

If possible, include the page's main search phrase in the first paragraph, or as near to the top as you can, while still writing good content for your visitor.

Near Text End –

In the same way, include the page's main search phrase in a paragraph near the end of the page. Your page should have at least 400 words, but pages can be longer. If you have a longer page, you can easily stick the phrase into the text somewhere in the middle.

GOOGLE-HAPPY PAGES

By some mysterious process, Google has decided that reputable sites have the following pages, and since you want to be a "reputable" site, you'll want to include the following pages.

You don't usually want to clutter up your main navigation bar with these, because they're not of interest to most human visitors. So you'll stick them either *below* main navigation bar pages, or

---

you'll stick these particular pages into some text navigation you load into the footer using a widget, if your theme has that ability.

Plugins make adding these Google-Happy pages pretty easy to do.

Site Map –

A site map can be created easily. Assuming you've installed and activated the Dagon Design Site Map plugin, just create a page called "Site Map," and using the html tab, enter the short code:
```
<!-- ddsitemapgen -->
```

Save the page, and when viewed, you'll see a nice site map. It will update automatically if you add or delete pages or posts (articles).

Terms and Conditions –

In the Resource section, I've included a file with some standard text that you can use for your Terms and Conditions page. Just paste in the text and save the page.

Privacy Policy –

A privacy policy page can be created easily. Assuming you've installed and activated the Privacy Policy plugin, just create a page called "Privacy Policy," and using the html tab, enter the short code:
```
<!-- privacy-policy -->
```

Save the page, and when viewed, you'll see a nice privacy policy.

Contact Us / About Us –

The about-us page would be used where a bio of yourself, or your company, would be in order, so that's optional. A contact-us page should always be used, and don't put your naked email on the page, because spammers collect nearly all their emails to spam from naked email addresses appearing on websites. Use the Dagon Design Form Generator plugin instead.

In the Resource section, you'll find a text file with sample "contact us" boilerplate text, and the Dagon Design Form Generator short code:

```
<!-- ddfm1 -->
```

Save the page and when viewed it will prettily list your contact information and provide a nice email box for anyone to send you a message, with a simple "captcha" to stop the robots. (A "captcha" is a graphic image that can be seen by the human eye, but not by a computer robot; the image is usually some text or random numbers that the human can see, and must type into a box, to prove that the form is being filled out by a real person.)

Articles Archive –

Google doesn't really care whether or not you have an archive of the articles (posts) you create, but Google does like to see a larger site, and the archive creates an additional page which updates automatically whenever you add a page or a post. Plus, it may be helpful for users, and adds keyword richness … so use it.

Create a page called "Article Archive," and in the html tab, enter the Simple Archive shortcode:

```
<!-- simple_archive -->
```

Save the page, and when viewed it will present a nice listing of all the pages and posts.

Plugins Settings –

The plugins mentioned above often have a few settings you need to make. For example the Form Generator plugin needs to know where to email the contents of the email form. The Form Generator doesn't reveal what your email address really is. That's a good thing, because a naked email address on your website is a guaranteed spam-collector magnet.

The Privacy Policy plugin also needs to know what email address you want to display for visitors' contact purposes on the Privacy page. However, very few humans will ever use this email address – which is in plain sight and thus visible to spam-collector robots – and so I suggest that you make up some email address on gmail for this purpose, because the email arriving at this address will universally be spam.

So to provide settings that different plugins may need, look in the left column of Wordpress, and see the plugin names under "settings" and click on each plugin's name, to open the panel for each plugin's settings. Most of the settings can be left on defaults, but you'll see a few things you need to enter into the boxes there.

DRIP SITE-CONTENT REGULARLY

Google likes to see large sites, and Google believes that sites which change are important, and when they change frequently, they are even more important.

So don't just set up your site and disappear. Set up some articles, and use the "scheduling" feature built into Wordpress to make these articles appear over time. The more of them, and the more frequently, the better.

But it's better to have one every month for the next year than to have twelve in the next two weeks and then nothing.

OTHER: TEXT NAVIGATION

Once upon a time, text navigation was added, usually at the bottom of the page, for those poor people who didn't have a browser that would show pictures.

Those days are gone, and today's visitor doesn't really need text navigation ... but realize that those text navigation links give you a great opportunity to tell Google what all the pages are about.

For example, on a helicopter tours website we built, the text navigation words are used to help Google understand the different kind of helicopter services we're outlining on the website. Take a

look at the text navigation near page bottom on this site:
  http://lakeshastahelicopter.com

This website had the problem that we needed to describe a number of different services, all related to the main keyword phrase "helicopter" and/or "helicopter tours." We also wanted to flag several "geography/location" keywords. We ended up with the following text navigation at the bottom of the page:

> Lake Shasta Helicopter Tours * Mt. Shasta Helicopter Tours * Airborne Mountain and Lake Photography * Helicopter Wedding and Wedding Planner Resources * Helicopter Pilots * Helicopter Flights Newsletter * Helicopter Recreation Articles * Helicopter Flight Costs * Northern California Information * Tourist Attractions * Terms * Privacy * Site Map (each of these links to some page or post on the site)

You can see how we used a core keyword for each service, and a page or a post was created for each of those services. Then the text navigation with keyword-rich links was simply added to the bottom of every page, using an automatic feature built into the particular Wordpress theme we created for this site.

OTHER: INTERNAL ANCHOR-TEXT

In addition to some place to insert text navigation, on various posts and pages on your website, you will have opportunity to refer to other pages on your own website. Whenever you do, be sure to use keyword-rich words inside the link.

OTHER: USING GOOGLE RELATED-PHRASES

Use the "related phrases" display in Google search to discover the subjects that Google *already* believes to be related, and then create additional pages or posts (articles) on these subjects. On each of those pages, pop the article's main keyword into Google to uncover the phrases that Google now finds related to this new article's main keyword, and stick some of those related phrases into the article.

Google finds this convincing, because you're telling Google what Google already believes to be true.

OTHER: MBP PING OPTIMIZER PLUGIN

I didn't mention this plugin among the essential plugins, but if you want to get extra mileage every time you add an article, then install and activate the MBP Ping Optimizer page, and then in the Resource section copy the "Big Ping" list I've provided. Paste this big ping list into the box under the Ping Optimizer's settings.

Now every time you post a new article, whether newly written or scheduled for future publication, then when the article is published, a large notification will be sent out to a number of "ping" directories. Don't ask me to explain these to you, but it's a good thing.

OTHER: XML SITEMAP PLUGIN

Similarly, I didn't mention the XML Sitemap plugin. This plugin creates a sitemap, but not one for the humans to see. Rather this is in a format that Google likes to read, because it makes Google's job of scanning your website faster and easier.

Further, whenever you publish a new article, this plugin will directly contact Google, Bing, and Yahoo, to let them know there's new content.

Remember, Google likes to see sites growing and changing. This plugin makes sure that Google knows promptly about the growing and changing that just occurred on your site.

This plugin also has one box in its settings where you need to insert page numbers for pages you don't want Google to display, like your "get-free-book" page for example. (The page number is visible in the address at page top when you are editing a page.)

OTHER: WP-SUPERCACHE PLUGIN

One thing that Google counts toward your score is whether your web pages load fast.

If they load fast, then Google knows that the search users will be happy, and so you get points when your pages are fast-loading. This may account for as much as 10% of your "score," according to Matt Cutts, the Google PR dude.

The WP-Supercache plugin does only one thing: it makes a Wordpress website load faster.

OTHER: RICH CONTENT – AUDIO, VIDEO, PICTURES

Google values content, and adding audio or video or pictures adds content and gives you lots more keywording opportunities.

Humans value entertainment and easy comprehension, and adding audio or video or pictures make your site more interesting, easier to understand, and they'll spend more time on your site looking and listening. It's a good thing.

OTHER: SIZE MATTERS

The larger your site is, the more important you must be, according to Google.

The easy way to make your site larger in the beginning is to add the Google-Happy pages, and a couple of articles. The easy way to make your site grow larger and larger over time is to schedule future-published articles.

OTHER: CHANGE MATTERS

Google thinks that sites which change must be important, because they must be more up-to-date. Therefore you want to change over time. Used future-scheduled articles (posts) to do this. They don't need to be long, perhaps 300-400 words is enough.

Got an article that's quite a bit longer? Great! Chop it into smaller parts, and schedule the parts to be published. In the eyes of Google this is now *several* pages and not just one.

Remember that publishing only one article a month is better than publishing 12 the first month and then none.

FINALLY: CONSIDER YOUR SITE VISITORS

Take some time and imagine that *you* are a visitor to your site.

- Would you *trust* the site?

- Would you feel comfortable giving your credit-card number to this site?

- Is this site useful?

- Is this site easy to navigate?

- Can you find what you need? Find what you want to know?

In general, when you create a website that's really attractive to your particular customer, and which is very useful for your particular customer, you will tend to have a customer who is happy about you. Just like an attractive and useful brochure, your website is presenting an experience of you to your customer, and he will react to what you're providing him.

And, when you take this approach, you will tend to create a site that makes Google happy at the same time. And when Google happy, everybody happy.

TRAFFIC: HOW TO GET BACKLINKS

"He who is truly great does not upon the surface dwell, but on what lies beneath." — *Tao Te Ching*

THE IMPORTANCE OF BACKLINKS

Matt Cutts, the Google PR dude, has stated that Google bases about 60% of your "score" on the backlinks that point to your site. A backlink is a link on some site out there on the Internet, and that link points to your site. It might point to your domain name, your home page, or to some page inside your site.

When you analyze the positioning of competing sites on a Google results page, sometimes you will find a site which doesn't have much page rank, and doesn't have the key phrase in the domain name or the page name, and yet it's ranking well.

Often if you'll check out the number of backlinks – Hint: Yahoo's backlinks count is more complete than Google's backlinks count – you will discover that the reason that the site is ranking so well is because it has lots of "good quality" backlinks.

ABOUT "ANCHOR TEXT"

Let's say your site is http://BlueNecktiesRUs.com and you are about to engage in a project to get a bunch of backlinks out there on the Internet, all pointing to your website.

Now a link usually has two parts. One part is what the web surfer sees. For example, all those links that just say "Click Here," the web surfer is just seeing "Click Here." The words that the web surfer sees are called the "anchor text." (For historical reasons, certain types of links were originally referred to as "anchors" and so it came to be that the text used in the link came to be called "anchor text.")

And the other part of the link is the http:// part. (Now the "http:// is just an instruction to your browser that the contents should be displayed using the "hyper text transfer protocol," which means "display as a web page.")

The http:// part may be pointing to your domain name, which will display your home page, or the http:// part may be pointing to some page down within your website:

http://BlueNecktiesRUs.com

http://BlueNecktiesRUs.com/great-necktie-selection/

http://BlueNecktiesRUs.com/products/narrow-and-skinny-neckties/

And, depending upon how the link was set up, the web-surfer will perhaps see this entire link, or the web-surfer may simply see words, like "Click Here" or "Great Neckties" or your business name "Blue Neckties R Us, Inc." or some call to action like "get skinny neckties here."

When *you* set up a link, in general you get to select both the text to appear ("anchor text") and the url to which it will point to (home url, or some sub-page).

What will help you the most?

BEST BACKLINKS FOR MAXIMUM "GOOGLE JUICE"

As you set up backlinks – we'll discuss how to do that in the rest of this chapter – here are some general guidelines:

1) Send about half the backlinks to your home page, your main url

2) Send the other half to specific sub-pages

3) Occasionally make a link that just points to your URL; that is, the web surfer will see the link itself as the "anchor text." The websurfer will see http://BlueNecktiesRUs.com

4) But most of the time, make sure that the anchor text is a good keyword phrase. For example, if pointing to your main URL, the anchor text might say "Neckties" or "Blue Neckties" or "Buy Neckties Here."

5) Do not make all the anchor text the same. Perhaps 60% should be right on your most important key phrase, and then another 30% of your backlinks should have anchor text which is just slightly different than your most important key phrase, and the remaining 10% of your backlinks should have links with some completely different phrases than your most important key phrase.

If you do it this way, then all of your backlinks out there on other folks' sites will look "natural." That's how natural or "organic" links occur, so that's what Google should see.

Now ... where should these backlinks appear, for maximum benefit?

HARMONY OF THE LINKING SITE

It's best if the web page on which your backlink appears is on the same subject, or a related subject, to the page on your website to which the backlink points.

In other words, if you had a YouTube video, and that video was about "How to tie a Windsor Knot in your Necktie," and you had a backlink there in the YouTube description, and that backlink pointed to a page on your website that said "How to Tie a Windsor Knot," that would be very good harmony between the backlink page and the target page on your site.

If you can get backlinks from other websites that are about neckties, that would be great. Next best might be backlinks from other websites that were about clothing, suits, dress shirts, cufflinks, and sports coats.

It probably won't hurt you terribly if you get some links from Uncle Fred's website about his accounting services, especially if the link occurs in some paragraph about dressing well, but try to avoid getting backlinks from: (a) porn sites; (b) scam sites; (c) real small sites; (d) sites which are clearly unimportant; (e) dead sites which haven't changed in five years; and try to avoid getting a *majority* of your backlinks from sites and pages which are unrelated to your website.

A few handfuls of backlinks from important, large, and related-subject pages are worth more than dozens and dozens from low-value sites. And getting backlinks from porn or scam sites can damage your rating.

EXAMPLE: ARTICLE DIRECTORIES

There is an entire method of online marketing called "Article Marketing." It's been around for a number of years and it still works well. Here's how it works –

There are a number of "article directories" online. People write articles and place them on these directory sites, where the articles are now free for the taking. So for example, if you were a guy who had a site about woodshop safety, you could go on one of these article directory sites, and get some great, free content for your website.

For example, I'm looking right now for "woodshop safety" on one of the major article directories, and all these articles immediately appear on the first page of my search –

- Three Essential Woodshop Safety Rules to Keep You from Harm

- Woodshop Safety – Embarrassing Injury Confessions

- Miter Saw Kickback & Woodshop Safety

- Safety Woodshop Ideas

- The Ultimate Guide to your Most Dangerous Woodworking Power Tools

- Woodworking Safety Tips

- Five Ways to Avoid Woodworking Accidents

- A Clean Woodshop is a Safe One

So I might take some of these articles and I can "reprint" them on my website, so I'm getting relevant, free content for my website on the subject of woodshop safety.

There's only one catch: And that is that I am required to print the *entire* article, which includes a "bio box" about the writer. And you can bet your bippy that the article writer put a couple of handy backlinks to *his* site into the bio box.

So the article writer is creating backlinks to his website. He gets an initial, high-value backlink as soon as he publishes the article, because the articles directory site is an important, large, frequently-changing site, and the page where his article appears is on the same subject (because he wrote the content for that page; he wrote the article himself). For those reasons, the very first backlink he gets is valuable. And if he never got any more than that, he's created one very high quality backlink, completely under his own control, and all he had to do was write the article of perhaps 400 words and then load it onto the articles directory site.

But if his article turns out to be popular, and other webmasters find it and choose to publish it on their websites, then the article writer could get an additional backlink every time the article is republished. The content will still be in harmony with the backlink, because the article writer wrote the article and therefore has complete control over the content of the article, and the content of the article becomes the content of the page where the backlink appears ... so if you do it right, the page content, the anchor text of the backlink, and the content of the target page on your website will all be harmonious.

Article writing has worked for many years, and should continue to work for a long time to come. If you know the tricks, you can also reuse the content of your article –

- You can use the article on *your own* site. Why not? Set it to future publish, and increase your site's size and show Google how your site grows and changes.

- You can take the article and perform an operation called "article spinning" on the article, and from the one article you could create ten, twenty, or a hundred articles on the same subject but with different words ... and you could place these "other" articles onto other article directories, or on other types of sites (discussed below).

So that you can see some typical articles, here is one of my author accounts on one of the largest Article Directories, using one of my "pen names," which is "Trevor James":

http://ezinearticles.com/?expert=Trevor_James

To learn more about article marketing, watch the demonstration videos, see the Resource section of this book to find article-marketing materials, and visit this site:

http://simply-free-article-spinner.com

This is a site I sponsor that contains online article spinning software that you can use. (Registration required, but site and spinner usage is free.)

EXAMPLE: SQUIDOO

In addition to article directories, there are a number of sites that contain content, but which are not designed for visitors to re-use the articles. These sites hope to contain lots and lots of informative material, and for some mysterious reason, the pages on this particular site are called "lenses."

Why do authors invest the time to write these "free information" pages? Because, once again, when you write one of these pages, you can insert backlinks to your own websites. Here are a couple of my own Squidoo articles:

http://www.squidoo.com/helicopter-adventure-travel-in-northern-california

http://www.squidoo.com/the-chapman-stick

In each of these pages (they call them "lenses") you'll see keyword-rich content, and you'll find backlinks to the website(s) I wish to promote.

Because Squidoo is a large, authoritative site, and because each page ("lens") is on a subject harmonious to my website pages being linked to, these are valuable backlinks.

The cost? No cost, except that sites like Squidoo usually need longer articles than the normal "article directory" does, and so it takes a little longer to write these longer articles.

EXAMPLE: GOOGLE KNOL

There are a number of these "information" sites (some of them are called "document" sites) on which you can set up an account, write pages, and include backlinks to your own sites. There are quite a few, not necessarily well known, like wikidot, wet paint, hubpages.

However, we know that Google really likes its own sites, so you might want to consider Google Knol. This is a knowledge site – a "knol" is deemed to be one unit of knowledge; cute, huh? – and as you can see, you can simply contribute information on some subject which falls within your expertise, and you can include a backlink to your (hopefully related) website.

EXAMPLE: BLOG COMMENTING

As you've probably noticed, many weblogs – and many sites that have "articles" – will allow comments. The site owner likes comments because it gets users to help him create a growing and changing site, and if he has a significant following, this is a valid way to stay in touch and connected to buyers and prospects and other followers.

Some blogs allow comments, and some do not. There are individual sites sitting on their own domain names, and there are also very large "free website" blogs, including Blogger and Wordpress.com, where anyone can sign up for one or many "blogs" and so create pages to satisfy their ego, or to serve the same purpose as the article directories, Squidoo, or Google Knol.

Now if you can locate a blog (or a site with "articles") which is on a harmonious subject to your web page, and if that site allows comments, then you can create a backlink on their website that links back to you.

<u>Best Blog-Posting Practice</u> –

Typically, the comment-requesting site will ask for your name, an email (not shown to site visitors), a box in which to type your comment, and a URL.

Typically, if the comment is approved – sometimes this is automatic, and sometimes a human looks at it first – then your comment will appear showing your name and the comment. Further, your name will be a hot link to your URL.

Now if your website is about Barbecue, and your name is John Smith, then the fact is that "John Smith" is not very good anchor text as a link pointing to http://bostonbarbeque.com.

So why not enter your "Name" as "Boston Barbecue John" or "Great Barbecue Dude?"

That way, when the comment is approved, there's a live link to your website, and it's got anchor text which is telling Google that your website is about barbecue. Good idea?

<u>Please Do Not Spam People's Blogs</u> –

"Spam" means some communication which is was not requested and is unwanted by the person receiving it. The name comes from a Monty Python television skit where a fellow walks into an English "fish & chips" shop, and wants to buy some food. In this particular fish & chips shop, every single item on the menu contained the meat product with the trademark "Spam" as one of the ingredients. So no matter what he ordered, he was going to receive some Spam on the plate, and he didn't really want Spam.

The word "spam" then came to mean, originally, an email you didn't request and you don't want. But it also means to receive a comment on your blog or forum that you weren't seeking and don't want.

So for example, if you have a blog about how to take care of little babies, and I come along and post a blog comment that talks about how to make big money in the commodities market – that's spam to the blog owner. Likewise, if you have a blog about making money in the commodities market, and I post a comment that's unresponsive to your article, and I plug my book about how to raise bees, that's spam on your commodities blog.

But if you have a commodities blog, and I make a responsive and useful comment (or even ask a relevant question) and I can make my comment on the subject, and useful. It's not spam.

Spamming is unkind, selfish, and generally speaking it won't work either, because most blog owners will see your comment as being valueless to their readers, so they'll toss out your comment, and you wasted your time for nothing.

What's the right approach? Simple. Post useful information. If you don't know any useful information from within your own expertise, look up something useful ... or pass on commenting on that particular blog today. Find some other harmonious blog where you *do* have something valuable to contribute, and comment that.

Where to Find Appropriate Blogs?

In the Resource section of this book, you'll find information about how to use the CopyDragon special-purpose Blog-Locator Search Engine. This will enable you to find blogs (and sites) that allow commenting, on most subjects.

EXAMPLE: FORUM POSTS AND FORUM SIG

When you have a website, and you're active within some area, you may naturally locate some online forums where like-minded people gather to talk about this particular subject.

For example, for the specialty guitars that I manufacture (http://megatar.com) there is an online forum called Tappistry forum, where musicians around the world can visit online. What they all have in common is the unusual method of play (called two-handed tapping, or touchstyle) whereby you touch the strings to play them, and most of them play the specialty instruments containing both bass and melody strings, so you can, in effect, play bass and guitar at the same time, playing much like a piano player would do. This forum is located at http://tappistry.org/forum/

To find relevant forums, you can simply search for the subject of your interest, plus the word "forum," and quickly find forums related to the subject of your website. You can join the forum, lurk a few days to get the feel for it, and then begin to post and ask questions, and take part in the discussion.

Naturally, where it's appropriate, you can insert links to your own pages. You'd be wise to avoid a hard-sell, and be sure to check the forum's rules, because some of them are totally lunatic that no selling is to be done.

But in any event, on almost any forum, you are permitted to set up a forum "signature" which is some bit of text that will be appended to the end of your posts. And generally, inside that signature you can put a live link to your website(s).

See your forum's rules and its "control panel" for details that apply.

Popular forums tend to be large, ever-growing, and changeable, and so they tend to be important in the eyes of Google. So any backlink from a reputable forum is likely to help your site.

OTHER BACKLINKS METHODS

There are many, many, many methods for getting valuable backlinks.

It is beyond the scope of this book to cover the field. However, the basic methods given in this chapter will give you a start, and you'll be ahead of 98% of all the do-it-yourselfers in the world, who generally don't know how to get backlinks, and they don't know that they should, and they may not even know what a backlink is.

When CopyDragon webwriters provides a "done-for-you" solution for a client, we access a very wide variety of quality backlinking sources, with proper anchor-text, for maximum "Google Juice." To give you an idea of the places where powerful backlinks can be placed, here is a list:

- Social-site profiles (Facebook, MySpace, Linked-In)

- Authority Sites like Wikipedia

- How-to Sites like eHow, Ask, and Yahoo Answers

- Writing "guest" articles for important industry websites

- Requesting backlinks and swaps from others in your industry

- Video sites like YouTube and Vimeo

- Classified ads like Craigslist

- Press Releases

- Creating online radio station programs

- "Pinging"

- "RSS" directories (stands for "Real Simple Syndication")

- "Bookmarking" sites

- Aggregator sites like Social Monkee

- Creating "Link Wheels" of linked articles which then point to your site

- Pay-Per-Click through Adwords

- Link buying and Banner-ad buying

- And lots, lots more!

In the Resource section of this book, I'll provide information from which you can expand your backlinking opportunities. But for now, the specific examples given will get you started and boost you past 98% of the other do-it-yourselfers in the world.

ORGANIC BACKLINKS (BY ACCIDENT)

In the great scheme of things, let us not forget the free backlinks … what people give us because our site provides something of value. Our own "article spinner" website has held up very well in the search-engine rankings over the last number of years, in spite of later, better-financed competitors, and that's largely because the free service we provide is useful, and so many how-to-do-it teachers about online marketing have sent their followers to our website, and have so created valuable backlinks on their own large websites pointing to us.

The more valuable and interesting your site to the humans, the more you'll get these free backlinks. Now you have no control over what they use for anchor text. They will tend to say either your business name or your domain name, but no problem. It's free, and it's good.

MONITORING BACKLINKS

If you wish to see what backlinks are coming to you, there are a number of ways to do so. But since they change from time to time, I suggest you simply do a Google search on "how to count backlinks?"

(This complete-sentence method of search seems to work well. It's treating Google as if Google were a "Magic 8 Ball," and you'll be given quite a bit of information about how to calculate the number of backlinks to your website. Warning: all the methods will arrive at a different answer, most likely. You're not so much interested in the hard number, as in creating an *increase* in the number.)

Your ongoing monitoring may be better served by these two methods:

a) If you have a "cPanel" back door on your website, see if you have access to something called "Webalyzer" which tells you about the number of unique visitors coming to your website. Of course, some of them will be search-engine robots, but you're interested to see how much you can *increase* the number of visitors with your online promotion and backlinking efforts.

b) Google has a free service called "Google Alerts," and this can be good to keep track of new online mentions of your own domain, your business name, your competitors, and/or the subject of your business. (This will also uncover blogs and forums with posts harmonious and related to your site.)

FINAL WORDS

On-site Search-Engine Optimization is a little quicker and easier than backlinks, but you'll need to do both to get the best results from Google. If you've chosen your keywords and your domain name wisely, if you've done a decent job of making your site coherent and focused, and if you begin an ongoing campaign of creating relevant and focused backlinks, you should see your website rise in the Google ratings, and hopefully you can get on the front page.

If you just *cannot* get well ranked in Google, then you'll need to create effective systems to *send* visitors to your website. But in most cases, especially with a local business who puts its geographic keywords into the domain, it is still possible to rank well and so appear in front of people who wish to buy.

Backlinks create both focus ... and power.

CONCLUSION

These days, running a local business can take a lot of work. The information in this book can make that local business more profitable. Here are the three things for you to take away:

1. There are two universes. You will be operating in both if you're doing any kind of commerce in today's times. In fact, having a working, profitable web presence is often a "screaming need" for a local business, if you wish to safeguard and maximize your profits.

2. Twenty percent of things done will accomplish eighty percent of results. So what I'm providing in this book is a twenty-percent system of the most workable solutions and approaches we've tested at CopyDragon webwriters for our own websites and those of our customers. The method given in this book is not the only possible method. But it's the best one we've seen, and has worked well for our own sites and those of our clients. The method is called …

3. The Three-Step Marketing formula. In either universe, you'll employ these three steps – Location, Conversation, Traffic – in that order.

In this book, I've given you the most-applicable techniques to create an effective and workable online-marketing system for your local business.

If you want the *most powerful* online-marketing system possible, then hire a professional marketing-design company which understands marketing online and off, to optimize your website to appeal strongly to your customers, to engage your customers with powerful conversation systems, and to persuade Google that your company is just magnificent.

But if you're doing your own work, then follow the specific techniques given in this book to apply the Three-Step Marketing formula online, and this will enable you to create an online presence that will work better than the websites of 98% of the do-it-yourselfers around the world.

These are tried and tested methods. And you really have no option these days. You really *must* operate both online and off, even if you're a "strictly local" business.

You can do it.

Here's to your success!

Sixty-Eight Useful Resources for You

"The only resource which is limited in your world is time." — *Perryman G. Davies*

Here you will find resources you can use to implement the step-by-step approach to creating a powerful Three-Step Marketing online system for your business.

Free Access to complete Step-by-Step Video Series

To assist you in applying the step-by-step guidelines in this book, we have created a companion video series, and in an exclusive "Members Area" on our book website, we provide these videos at no cost to purchasers of this book.

Please go to http://MarketingOnlineClearAndSimple.com. There it will offer to sell you the videos, along with a pdf download of this book, readable on any computer.

But since you have already purchased this book on Amazon, Nook, the iBook store, or elsewhere, you can register for a FREE access to the videos in the Members Area, and you'll get a copy of the pdf book as well, at no charge.

Just act as if you were buying the book on the website – but enter the Coupon Code (given below) on the shopping cart, and click the "apply" button – and the price will change to ZERO, so it costs you nothing.

Complete your zero-cost "purchase," and you can then choose a username and password for the membership (videos) area.

When you log-in to the Members Area, all the videos will be available to you, plus we'll send additional materials (for free) to help you easily create an online presence making your business ever more powerful, for greater profits.

YOUR COUPON CODE:

To get your bonus copy of the book in pdf format, and access to the complete set of how-to videos *for free* on our shopping cart:

Enter this Coupon Code:

"MKTGBOOKVIDS"

KEYWORD RESEARCH

Google: Search --
http://google.com (add 'related searches')

Google: External Keywords tool --
https://adwords.google.com/select/KeywordToolExternal

Google: Insight --
http://www.google.com/insights/search/

Seo Quake --
http://www.seoquake.com/

 Seo Quake how-to guide --
http://www.seoquake.com/pages/guide.php

KEYWORD RESEARCH TOOLS

If you are a do-it-yourselfer, and you only have one website to create, then the above free resources will probably be enough. However, if you intend to become a professional, you may want to invest in professional keyword tools. Here are two of the best, that we use at CopyDragon webwriters:

Micro Niche-Finder --
http://voltos.us/MNF (recommended, the simpler of the tools)

Market Samurai --
http://voltos.us/MKTSAMURAI (more features)

ARTICLE ON ANALYZING COMPETITION'S LINKS
Famous Bloggers: "What Link Builders are Not Telling You" --
http://www.famousbloggers.net/link-builders-seo.html

DOMAIN RESEARCH
Psychic Whois --
http://psychicwhois.com

Rewordio.us
http://rewordio.us

REGISTRARS
eNom --
http://voltos.us/ENOM

NameCheap --
http://voltos.us/NAMECHEAP

HOSTING COMPANIES
If you have hired CopyDragon webwriters to create an online automatic-selling system for you, usually we provide free hosting for a period of time on our own webservers, with backup both locally, and to a distant city, and on our office backup systems.

However, if you are creating your own website, here is an inexpensive hosting company which generally has a good reputation. However, be aware that, with hosting companies, generally low cost also means they'll do very little hand-holding to help you figure things out; so if you need a lot of guidance, arrange for somebody knowledgeable to assist you if you wish to take advantage of a low-cost hosting company.

HostGator --
http://voltos.us/HOSTGATOR

WORDPRESS SOFTWARE
Do NOT get a free website on Wordpress.**com**, but DO get free Wordpress software from Wordpress.**org**. Note that your hosting company can probably provide the Wordpress software, either already installed for you, or they'll have a cPanel with Fantastico, which enables you to install Wordpress with just a few clicks. (This is covered on the free how-to videos.)

The Wordpress Organization --
http://Wordpress.org

WORDPRESS THEMES
Wordpress Themes are packages of code and graphics which can make your website look this way or that way. A theme can be installed in just a few clicks, and this ability to select your website's appearance so as to captivate your target customer is one of the powerful advantages of using the Wordpress software as the best general website-building approach.

As discussed, you can find a number of fairly good free themes available for Wordpress; however the very best theme designers can make money selling their themes, and so it follows that paid themes are often more powerful and attractive than free ones.

If you have a done-for-you solution from CopyDragon, we have purchased commercial rights to all of these themes, and so any of these themes can be used on your website.

Wordpress.Org (free themes) --
http://Wordpress.org   (choose "extend," and then "themes")

Refined Theme --
http://voltos.us/REFINED   (this was the sample theme used in the how-to video)

Elegant Themes --
http://voltos.us/ELEGANT

Woo Themes --
http://voltos.us/WOO

StudioPress Themes --
http://voltos.us/STUDIOPRESS

WORDPRESS PLUGINS

Just as Wordpress themes can change the appearance of your
website, so can Wordpress plugins add new functionality. Many
great plugins are free, though now and again, it's worth the money
to buy a paid plugin. The plugins in this list are the ones we find
useful over and over again.

Backup Buddy --
http://voltos.us/BACKUP

All free:
Dagon Design Form Mailer (a contact-us form) --
Dagon Design Sitemap Generator --
Exclude from Navigation --
Google XML Sitemaps --
Kahi's Notes --
MaxBlogPress Ping Optimizer --
My Page Order --
Privacy Policy --
Simple Archive Generator --
WP-Supercache --
Yost Wordpress SEO --
http://Wordpress.org (choose "extend," then "plugins")

SHORTCODES AND TEXT FOR PLUGINS

Several of the plugins are made to work by typing a short code onto
the page (using the "html" tab, not the "visual" tab). And a couple of
your "Google Happy" pages need some text. Here's a convenient list
of these items ...

Contact Us page, text and short code for DD Form Generator –
(enter with html tab, not the visual tab) –
Thank you for visiting the XXXXXXX website.

If you wish to contact us, here's how --

<ul><li>By Mail:

YOUR BUSINESS NAME

YOUR STREET ADDRESS

CITY, STATE ZIP USA</li>

<li>By Telephone:

(NNN) NNN-NNNN</li>

<li>By Email:</li></ul>

<!-- ddfm1 -->

Sitemap Generator shortcode --
  <!-- ddsitemapgen -->

Privacy Page shortcode --
  <!-- privacy-policy -->

Simple Archive shortcode --
  <!-- simple_archive -->

Boilerplate Text for "Terms and Conditions" page --
http://voltos.us/TERMS

Mailing-List Manager Companies
If you think you may need a shopping cart integrated with your
mailing list down the road, then use: Auto Web Business --
http://voltos.us/AUTOWEBBIZ

If you think you'll never need a shopping cart (or you plan to simply sell some individual items using PayPal) and this never needs to be integrated with your mailing list, then use: Aweber -- http://voltos.us/AWEBER

EXAMPLES OF FREEBIES AND EMAIL-CAPTURE SYSTEMS
CopyDragon.com – free 17-issue email briefing course – http://CopyDragon.com

KlamathRanchResort.com – free RV camping guide – http://klamathranchresort.com

BeingHappyToday.com – free mental health made easy – http://beinghappytoday.com

Megatar.com – free two-handed tapping book (guitar method) – http://megatar.com

LakeShastaHelicopters.com – free helicopter-touring guide – http://lakeshastahelicopters.com

EXAMPLES OF FACEBOOK CONVERSATION SYSTEM
CopyDragon's Business Page (17-lesson online mktg course) – http://Facebook.com/CopyDragon

Two-Handed Tapping (playing method for guitar) – http://Facebook.com/TwoHandedTapping

EXAMPLE OF FORUM CONVERSATION SYSTEM
Tappistry.Org International Forum for Two-Handed Tapping – http://tappistry.org/forum/

STOCK PHOTOS FOR SITE GRAPHICS AND FREEBIE GRAPHICS
iStock Photo -- http://voltos.us/ISTOCK

Power Point Pix -- http://voltos.us/PWRPTPIX

GRAPHICS SOFTWARE
Paint.net – free graphics software for windows – http://paint.net

Snap a Shot – free screen-capture software for windows – http://www.nicekit.com

Snagit – a better screen-capture software for windows and mac – http://voltos.us/SNAGIT

VIDEO SOFTWARE
Jing – free computer-screen capture software – http://voltos.us/JING

Camtasia – powerful and easy to use, computer-screen capture software – http://voltos.us/CAMTASIA

Windows Movie Maker – video-mixing software, free with Windows

iMovie – video-mixing software, free with Macintosh

Vegas – Very powerful, and fairly easy to use. Save big by purchasing a previous version on EBay (still more features than you'll ever be likely to use) – http://voltos.us/VEGAS

INTERVIEWING TOOLS
If you will be interviewing anyone as part of creating content for your website or for article-writing – or you're creating content by having somebody interview *you* – then here are two recommended tools that we've found useful at CopyDragon webwriters …

Audio-Video Acrobat – for interviewing over the phone (or uploading files)
They'll also provide a nice player for either soundfiles (audio) or

video for showing the video on your web pages. Better than YouTube, because YouTube offers links that carry your site visitor away from you and off to YouTube. (Good for them; not for you.) http://voltos.us/AVACROBAT

Zoom H3 Digital Recorder – This is an easy-to-use small digital recorder, and with a modest memory card can record up to 12 hours of speech in decent quality, with easy download to your computer via USB cable. Easy to find on Amazon: http://voltos.us/ZOOMH3

RE-BRANDABLE SOFTWARE
Rebrand Software (buy it, brand it, give away as freebie) http://voltos.us/REBRAND

FILE-TRANSFER SOFTWARE
FileZilla – FTP (File-Transfer Protocol) software, free http://filezilla-project.org

BOOKS
Tested Advertising Methods, by John Caples – http://voltos.us/CAPLES

How to Build a Facebook Business Page, by Arthur Cronos – http://voltos.us/FBBIZPAGE

Six Deadly Copywriting Methods, by Jason Fladlien – One of these methods gives you an easy-to-follow formula for creating near-irresistible headlines. And then you get five more super-powerful insider copywriting methods. Jason is one of my gurus, and has a way of making complex things clear and simple. I recommend it. http://voltos.us/COPYWRITING

TEXT EDITORS
Dark Room, a blank-screen text editor, free – http://voltos.us/DARKROOM

NoteTab, my favorite text editor, quick and easy to use, best I've found –
http://voltos.us/NOTETAB

ARTICLE MARKETING
Article Marketing Made Easy (video training course) –
http://voltos.us/ARTICLEMKT

Five-Minute Article-Writing method, by Jason Fladlien – If you undertake using the "article marketing" method for creating backlinks and increasing traffic to your site, you might as well become skillful at creating articles quickly and easily. Here it is.
http://voltos.us/5MINARTICLES

Simply Free Article Spinner – write it once, spin it, publish many times – This website also has some downloadable content on the site, and when you sign up for the newsletter and freebies, you'll learn lots more about the traffic-creating method called "article marketing."
http://voltos.us/SPINNER

Smiley-Tech Article Spinner, Article-Distribution, and SEO System –
http://voltos.us/SMILEYTECH
http://voltos.us/REWRITER
http://voltos.us/SEO

OTHER RESOURCES
"Silence is Golden," an index page to hide contents of a directory –
http://voltos.us/SILENCE

The "Big Ping" list for MBP Ping Optimizer plugin –
http://voltos.us/BIGPING

Keyword Density Tool for webpages and article-writing –
http://voltos.us/KEYWDDENSITY

The CopyDragon "Blog-Locator" search engine –
http://voltos.us/BLOGFINDER

BACKLINKING INFORMATION
Expanded methods for uncovering additional powerful ways to get valuable backlinks (for increasing traffic to your website) – http://voltos.us/BACKLINK

THIS BOOK
"Marketing Online, Clear and Simple" is available at seminars taught by Arthur Cronos and other online-marketing teachers, and from the following online locations:

Amazon .com (print edition & kindle editions) – http://amazon.com

Barnes & Noble (nook book e-reader edition) – http://www.barnesandnoble.com

Apple iBookstore (iBook/iPad e-reader edition) – http://www.apple.com/itunes/ (coming soon)

The official book site (pdf version, and video series) – http://marketingtodayclearandsimple.com

"Done for You" service from CopyDragon.com

"The prayer of the monk is not perfect until he no longer recognizes himself or the fact that he is praying." — St. Anthony

---

Up to your Belt-Buckle in Alligators?

Fact: Almost every business owner and manager wants to get more income, and suspects that it would be possible using the power of the Internet.

Fact: Almost no business owner or manager ever manages to figure it out. Oh, they're smart enough. In fact, business owners and managers are *extremely* ingenious.

The problem is that most business owners and managers are up to their belt-buckles in the alligators of daily operations, juggling jobs and watching to see what's most profitable, and plugging leaks and fixing problems, all very quickly.

This leaves little time for the research, testing, and evaluating of a complex subject with a long learning curve ... a subject like "how to use the Internet to generate actual income."

Plus, the formulation of the project is usually wrong. We see that some business has a website, and we think, "I gotta get a website." But, as you have discovered in the pages of this book, having a website is only the first step. What you've learned about the Three-Step Marketing formula has revealed to you that a Conversation-Engagement system is needed, if you want to actually benefit from the folks who visit, and that it's also necessary to send some traffic to the website, just as your physical store needs to have plenty of visitors!

WHAT'S THE BEST USE OF YOUR TIME?

If you will invest the time, then you can absolutely succeed in applying the Three-Step Marketing formula as we've described it here, step by step. If you *only* get the first step done – creating a properly-built website – you will have made a major step forward.

However, if you'd like to *magnify* the power of your online presence, and to get more income SOONER rather than later, it could be that the best use of your time is to hire us, and let us do it for you. You'll not only save time, but the automatic-selling machine we build for you will be more powerful than what you can engineer on your own. Fact.

In other words, it might be more profitable for us to work in parallel with you. We'll create your online money machinery, while you stay focused on keeping your existing business profitable.

It's your call. If you'd like to schedule a free discovery session, simply contact me. I'd be delighted to hear from you!

Arthur Cronos
CopyDragon webwriters
1445 Ieka Street
Weed, CA 96094
(530) 938-1100
arthur@copydragon.com

ABOUT THE AUTHOR: ARTHUR CRONOS

"Farmer, pointing the way, with a radish." — Issa

Arthur Cronos was born in Visalia, California in 1944 during the Second World War, and grew up in a small town in Northern Texas.

He studied engineering and psychology in school, and has since made a life-long study of the mind and the unconscious mind, especially as applied to ordinary life — business, romance, music, marketing, and design projects.

Mr. Cronos has designed computers and machine-control systems, written accounting and film-editing software. He worked in Huntsville Prison, drove a truck on a wheat harvest from Texas to Nebraska, and worked in hotels in Dallas, Beverly Hills, St. Louis, and San Francisco.

For many years he made an advanced study of counseling methods in Dallas, St. Louis, Los Angeles, Spain, and southern England, as well as further study in San Francisco for 20 years.

He has designed and sold advanced telephone systems used in the answering service industry, written additive synthesis software for synthesizers, composed and recorded songs on piano and on touch-style guitars. He has been the featured speaker at National Trade Association meetings, giving talks on marketing methods, and has written a number of books (therapy, romance, music, marketing).

With several others he has designed specialty touch-style guitars, and operates a factory for the manufacture of the Mobius Megatar Touch-Style Guitar, in Northern California.

Mr. Cronos is currently lead copywriter with CopyDragon webwriters, a professional business writing / marketing design firm. More details here – http://copydragon.com

Mr. Cronos has always been fascinated by the mind and by the application of mental technologies to the everyday world in which we live, and how our world and our everyday lives can still be so very magical.

OTHER BOOKS AND RESOURCES FROM ARTHUR CRONOS & ASSOCIATES

DATING & ROMANCE:
Drowning in Dates –
http://voltos.us/DATING

MUSIC:
Mobius Megatar premium touchstyle basses –
http://megatar.com

Revolutionary design for two-handed touchstyle guitars –
http://zentapper.com

World-Wide forum for the two-handed tapping method of play –
http://tappistry.org

THERAPY, SELF-HELP, & SPIRITUALITY:
How to Capture Happiness in an Unhappy World –
http://beinghappytoday.com

How to Tune a Human –
http://howtotuneahuman.com

Spirit Guide Drawings –
http://spiritguidedrawingsmtshasta.com

Tantra Yoga Classes –
http://voltos.us/TANTRA

LIFE & ADVENTURE:
The Adventures of Bloggard –
http://bloggard.com

And here, from *The Adventures of Bloggard*, you'll find a little story for your entertainment ...

A STORY: "WIZARD IN A CAVE"

"To work magic is to weave the unseen forces into form" —
Starhawk

Henrietta, Texas, 1951. My mother played her nice radio in the evenings, and we listened to Green Lantern, the Phantom, the Great Gildersleeve, the Lone Ranger, and the Inner Sanctum. Not long after, television would arrive, stealing drama from the radio, but in those days radio was one story after another.

Hobby time went well with radio. For example, my mother was a great and wonderful crafts person, and made marvelous things. As we sat in the evening with one lamp turned on, she was making colored flower stencils on pillow cases.

I had a project too. She'd bought me a drawing toy called a "Magic Slate." This cardboard rectangle has a gray plastic sheet attached, and a pencil-shaped wooden stylus. With this stylus, you write or draw upon the gray sheet. Whenever it's filled up, or you get tired of it, just lift the sheet and all the writing vanishes, and you can start over. Oh, the sheer magic of it!

That night we were listening to Inner Sanctum, which was a scary show about some sort of bird or a bat. But I wasn't scared. My mom was making stencils and I was a Wizard in a Cave.

I saw an image clearly — to be a Wizard in a Cave — staying up late, by candle-light, and writing mystical things on the Magic Slate. The only problem was, I didn't know any mystical things to write.

I was staying up late. I had the Magic Slate. I was all set. I scribbled some words and alphabet things. ... But they were only the things I knew. It wasn't really magical. It made me kind of sad, having no mystical things to write.

This isn't much of a story. I don't even remember what happened to the bird or bat thing.

But there is this: I think that the Wizard in a Cave has been the guiding image of my life.

I was no good in sports, so I learned to be a wizard. I was fearful of girls, way too shy, so I tried to appear wizardly, intellectual, knowing magical things, wise. Haw! Seems silly, now. Seemed to make sense, then.

I'm writing this now, late at night. One lamp is on. I'm in my workshop, surrounded by magical contrivances. The musical instruments I design and build, and on which I can compose, play, and improvise. A library of books, on arcane subjects such as database design, music theory, and investment charting. Computers are here. On them I have written books, made pictures, calculated mystical things such as additive sine wave patterns.

It's late, I am no longer young, there's one lamp, and it's cave-like. Welcome, Arthur. You are now a Wizard in a Cave, writing mystical things.

It's been a long road, but to arrive at being a Wizard in a Cave is just the way I thought it would be. I know mystical things, and I can write them down here, on this erasable page. Now they are both hidden, and visible to wizards all over the Universe.

The funny thing is, the most mystical of these magical things are the plain truths of human experience, the stories we all share, the open secrets of mankind, the pain and joy of living, the gaining and the terrible, terrible losses. This is the truest magic.

Even a child knows some of this. I knew magic on that night, not recognizing it there before me. The magic was that night, the color of the light, the human dreams, and my mother making stencils of colorful paint, on pillow cases, making some beauty, for her home.

CONTACT INFORMATION

"The reason angels can fly is that they take themselves so lightly." — G. K. Chesterton

---

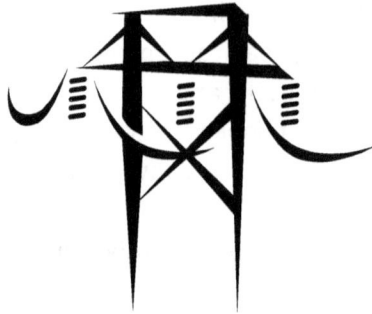

Powerline Press
Administrative Offices: 1445 Ieka Street
Weed, CA 96094 USA
Office: (530) 938-1100

http://CopyDragon.com

---

www.ingramcontent.com/pod-product-compliance
Lightning Source LLC
Chambersburg PA
CBHW050113210326
41519CB00015BA/3943